Dr. Ironside's Bible

Notes and Quotes from the Margins

H.A. Ironside

www.solidchristianbooks.com

2016

Contents

Introduction: A Coveted Treasure

A Coveted Treasure

In his biography of the late Dr. H. A. Ironside, Dr. E. Schuyler English mentions that Richard Bentley's description of Bishop Pearson can well be applied to Dr. Ironside: "The very dust of whose writings is gold."

It was my good fortune to come into possession of the Bible Dr. Ironside used for many years. Going over the voluminous notes it contains, one realizes that these comments and themes are indeed the very "dust of gold."

Without doubt the personal Bible of Dr. H. A. Ironside is a treasure. The flyleaf of the good-sized copy of the Authorized Version bears the record "Presented by Saints at Boston (Arlington Heights) Mass., Oct. 14, 1925." (This was Dr. Ironside's forty-ninth birthday.)

It is a day well remembered when this Bible, the most cherished possession of my library, became mine. The famous expositor was coming to the close of an eighteen-and-one-half-year ministry as Pastor of the Moody Memorial Church (which, by the way, is the record for a pastoral stay at this renowned church). Dr. Ironside had read thousands of books in his lifetime, and even though he had supplied schools and struggling preachers with hundreds of books, there were still some four thousand volumes to be taken from the shelves of his study and packed for shipment to Winona Lake, etc. It was my personal delight, as his assistant pastor, to spend several days helping him in this task.

One day, upon removing books from one of the lesser used compartments, my hands produced a fine old dust-covered Bible which was literally in pieces from extensive use. The cover bore the gold imprint "H. A. Ironside, Oakland, Calif." Immediately I asked the Pastor about the inscription.

"Yes," he replied, "that is the Bible I was preaching from when I received the call to be Pastor of the Moody Church. And I have used it for a good part of that ministry too."

Considering the fact that Dr. Ironside had been like a father to me, and was my hero as an expositor, I dared to mention that I should treasure such a possession for my very own.

"What would you do with it?" he asked. My answer was that I would treasure it as a memento of our association in the Word as father and son. Thus he gave it to me. Needless to say, I have cherished this keepsake, and have had the bookbinders restore the binding. It is now in safe condition to handle for study. My desire concerning this book is that I might share with others some of the treasure found therein.

The famous English poet, Matthew Arnold, declared, "Poetry is simply the most beautiful, impressive and widely effective mode of saying things, and hence its importance."

Many of us have experienced near nervous exhaustion, as some dear brother attempted the use of poetry from the pulpit. But ah, when H.A.I. would pause during a Bible exposition and quote a few lines which sweetly but surely cut to the heart, it was almost as if the Master Himself were speaking.

H.A.I, had such a love for message in meter that he wrote many hymns of praise himself. Who, in evangelical circles, has not heard the song "Overshadowed"? Let us look at one stanza and the chorus:

> How desolate my life would be,
> How dark and drear my nights and days,
> If Jesus' face I did not see
> To brighten all earth's weary ways.

> Chorus: I'm overshadowed by His mighty love,
> Love eternal, changeless pure,
> Overshadowed by His mighty love,
> Rest is mine, serene, secure;
> He died to ransom me from sin,

He lives to keep me day by day,
I'm overshadowed by His mighty love,
Love that brightens all my way.

H.A.I.'s Bible contains many poems, both penned and pasted in the flyleaves and margins. Reading a few of them will not begin to compare with hearing them quoted from his own lips, which are now silent awaiting "the blessed hope"—yet even in printed form his choice speaks the measure of the man himself!

My former association with Dr. Ironside was a most blessed experience. The call to be assistant pastor of the Moody Memorial Church was accepted in June 1947, which began for me a "Timothy" experience, the marks of which can never be erased from my life. For instance, sitting behind him as he preached verse by verse was like a seminary training in itself. Traveling with him to speaking engagements was always refreshing. My mind was alert trying to think up some theological question that might stump the "Old Apostle"; but his quick reply in Scripture quoting would leave me breathless. What a privilege to sit at the feet of such a Gamaliel! Many were the meals we ate together—that is, we started together but never finished together. He would be through a complete meal before I had started the second course, and would tell me at least three good stories before my dessert was finished.

What a giant of intellect and spirituality Dr. Ironside was! He would be found in his study most any morning at seven-thirty. His day included study of the Word; writing letters (in long hand) to missionaries, penning articles for publication, manuscripts for books, radio engagements, preaching and teaching engagements, personal interviews, and a short nap after the noon meal. The more I think about his capacity the more impossible his tasks seem to me. Yet I witnessed these things with my own eyes.

Many a professor of homiletics has been plagued with the perennial question that comes from new aspiring preachers, "What about H. A. Ironside, he doesn't use this system?" It is quite true that H.A.I, seemed to have homiletical rules that differed from those of Spurgeon and Talmadge; but did he or did he not get results? One day while driving my beloved Pastor to a preaching engagement, I broached the subject of homiletics. In our conversation I mentioned the names of professors who were looked upon as top bracket teachers in the field of homiletics, and waited for comment if forthcoming. It came. With a twinkle in his eye he said, "You know, it's a strange thing, but many of these men who can tell you how, were never able to do the job themselves."

Upon studying H.A.I.'s Bible one is brought face to face with the fact that he had a very concise way of explaining truth, as for example the few samples of his outlines and themes included in "Suggestive Themes from H.A.I.'s Bible."

A few moments of browsing through his Bible will quickly reveal H.A.I.'s devotional love for the Book, also his method of expounding it. He was probably the most famous exponent of verse-by-verse exposition of our generation. And literally thousands of sheep crowded the great Moody Church week after week for over eighteen years, because better pasture could not be found anywhere else.

H.A.I.'s manner of marking the Bible is a fascinating study in itself. In fact, all flyleaves are actually covered with sayings, poems, diagrams, illustrations, epitaphs, and even Chinese characters, which he studied for recreation. Here and there, he has noted some of the great themes of the Bible, which signified the power and effectiveness of his preaching. But perhaps the richest of the treasure is the reading of his choice comments scattered over some fifteen hundred pages of Scripture, as written by him in the margins.

This volume contains selections from the many marginal notes found in each of the Books of the great expositor's old Bible. If the reader will fit these notes with chapter and verse, he will find the map leading to buried treasure.

Herbert J. Pugmire, D.D., F.R.G.S.
Galilean Baptist Church
Dallas, Texas

Poems From The Flyleaves

At What a Cost

Chosen, redeemed, in the children's place,
Holy and blameless before His face,
Once guilty, ruined, and lost;
Not e'en doth the light of His presence show
A single stain—washed whiter than snow;
But, ah! at what a cost!

Not glittering gems, nor silver and gold,
Not worlds though teeming with wealth untold,
Could for our ransom suffice.
No, the Church of God was bought with the blood
Of the holy, spotless Lamb of God;
This, this was the costly price.

Oh wondrous truth! Deep in each breast
By the Spirit of God be it impressed,
And there by His power abide,
Grant, oh our God, that our life below
May brightly reflect the truths we know,
That Thou mayest be glorified.

M.A.S.

"Often I am tempted to flee my task
But that Strange Man upon the Cross
Bars my way and holds me back."

Terrell

"Bold infidelity; turn pale and die.
Beneath this stone four sleeping infants lie;
Say, are they lost or saved?
If death's by sin they sinned for they are here,
If Heaven's by works in Heaven they can't appear,
Reason, ah, how depraved!
Turn to the Bible's sacred page, the knot's untied.

They died, for Adam sinned;
They live, for Jesus died."

Epitaph on a tombstone over four children, in
St. Andrews Church Yard, Scotland

I hear a Voice you cannot hear,
Which says I must not stay.
I see a Hand you cannot see,
Which beckons me away.

I sometimes feel the thread of life is slender
And soon with me the labor will be wrought,
Then grows my heart to other hearts more tender,
The time is short.

D. M. Clark

The Hands of Christ

"The hands of Christ seem very frail
For they were broken by a nail;
But only they reach heaven at last
Whom those frail broken Hands hold fast."

J. R. Moreland

The following is pasted in the margin of H.A.I.'s Bible
beside Romans 6:16—"Obedience"

Make me a captive, Lord,
And then I shall be free;
Force me to render up my sword,
And I shall conqueror be.
I sink in life's alarms
When by myself I stand;
Imprison me within thine arms,
And strong shall be my hand.

My will is not my own
Till thou hast made it thine;
If it would reach the monarch's throne

It must its crown resign:
It only stands unbent
Amid the clashing strife
When on Thy bosom it has leant,
And found in Thee its life.

George Matheson

"Whoso hath felt the Spirit of the Highest
Cannot confound, nor doubt Him nor deny.
Yea, with one voice, oh world thou thou deniest
Stand thou on that side, for on THIS am I."

Workmen of God! oh, lose not heart,
But learn what God is like;
And in the darkest battlefield
Thou shalt know where to strike.

Thrice blest is he to whom is given
The instinct that can tell
That God is in the field when He
Is most invisible.

Blest too is he who can divine
Where real right doth lie,
And dares to take the side that seems
Wrong to man's blindfold eye.

Then learn to scorn the praise of men,
And learn to lose with God;
For Jesus won the world through shame,
And beckons thee His road.

As He can endless glory weave,
From what men reckon shame,
In His own world He is content
To play a losing game.

Faber

"Marvel not that Christ in glory
All my inmost heart hath won,
Not a Star to cheer my darkness
But a light beyond the sun.
I have seen the face of Jesus
Tell me not of ought beside,
I have heard the voice of Jesus
All my soul is satisfied.
In the radiance of the glory,
First I saw His blessed face,
And forever shall that glory
Be my home, my dwelling place."

"Ah! little I'll reck, when the journey is o'er,
Of the burdens and griefs I so dreaded, and bore—
They'll all be forgot as I enter the door.
With that light on my face, and that song in my ears
How small my regard for past troubles and fears,
While my harp makes the music I've longed for for years."

"When I am dying how glad I shall be
That the lamp of my life has been blazed out for Thee
I shall not regret one thing that I gave,
Money or time one sinner to save.
I shall not mind that the way has been rough;
That Thy blest feet led the way for me is enough;
When I am dying how glad I shall be
That the lamp of my life has been blazed out for Thee."

They're Dear to God

Oh that, when Christians meet and part,
These words were graved on ev'ry heart—
"They're dear to God!"
However wilful and unwise,
We'll look on them with loving eyes—
"They're dear to God!"
Oh, wonder!—to the Eternal One
Dear as His own beloved Son;
Dearer to Jesus than His blood,

10

Dear as the Spirit's fixed abode—
"They're dear to God!"

When tempted to give pain for pain,
How would this thought our words restrain,
"They're dear to God!"
When truth compels us to contend,
What love with all our strife should blend!
"They're dear to God."
When they would shun the pilgrim's lot
For this vain world, forget them not,
But win them back with love and prayer;
They never can be happy there,
If dear to God.

Shall we be there so near, so dear,
And be estranged and cold whilst here—
All dear to God?
By the same cares and toils opprest,
We lean upon one faithful Breast,
We hasten to the same repose;
How bear or do enough for those
So dear to God!

"I pass within the glory even now
Where shapes and words are not
For joy that passeth words, O Lord art Thou,
And bliss that passeth thought."

Quotations From The Flyleaves

"Remember the devil can wall you round, but he cannot roof you in."

—Hudson Taylor to Dan Crawford.

"If you must speak your mind, then mind how you speak."

"God is a substitute for everything, but nothing is a substitute for God."

"The gospel of Christ once heard is always the gospel which has been heard. Nothing can ever alter that."

—Alexander MacLaren.

"Deus Meus mea omnia." Motto of Francis d'Assisi

"When I was rich, I had God in everything; now I am poor and I have everything in God."

—Testimony of a ruined business man.

"I will place no value on anything I have or may possess except in relation to the kingdom of Christ."

—David Livingstone.

God has wonderful things to display if He could only get the show cases.

"Young man, attend to the voice of one who has possessed a certain degree of fame in the world, and who will shortly appear before his Maker: Read the Bible every day of your life."

—Samuel Johnson, when dying,
to a young gentleman who visited him.

"I am in the place where it is demanded of conscience and of God that I shall speak the truth; and speak it I will: impugn it whoso lists."

—John Knox in the pulpit of St. Giles.

A Few Suggestive Themes From H.A.I's Bible

Paul's Prayers

1. Prayer for knowledge. Eph. 1:17.

2. Prayer for power. Eph. 3:14.

3. Prayer of seven petitions. Col. 1:9-11.

4. Prayer for keen perception and fruits of righteousness in the believer. Phil. 1:9-11.

That Blessed Hope—Titus 2:13.

A happy hope because—

· Christ Himself is to return.

· The first Resurrection and the living changed.

· The redemption of the body.

· The believer to be rewarded.

· The earth to be blessed.

The Women of the Apocalypse

· Four of them—representing corporate bodies of people. Jezebel—The papal system.

· Woman clothed with the sun—Israel invested with fullness of governmental authority.

· Babylon—the great harlot—The future corrupt church after the Lord's return for His own.

· Bride of the Lamb—The Church glorified in heaven.

Salvation from first to last. Titus 3:7

Reformation not salvation. Judges 17, 18

The revelation of the rapture. 1 Thess.4.

Group Bible Study

10 questions on a chapter.

Information

1. Principle subject?

2. Leading lessons?

3. Best verse?

4. Principle persons?

5. Teaching about Christ?

Application

1. Example to follow?

2. Error to avoid?

3. Command to obey?

4. Promise to claim?

5. Prayer to be echoed?

Principles of Prophetic Interpretation

1. Recognition of the Prophetic Character of the Bible. Jehovah's challenge—things to come—Isaiah 41:21-23.

Israel, Jehovah's witness—Isaiah 43:8-12.

2. Recognition of the unity of the prophetic Word—

2 Peter 2:16-20; Isaiah 34:16.

3. The literal character and the symbolic distinguished.

Past prophecy literally fulfilled—so with future.

If symbolic, plainly indicated.

4. Threefold division of mankind.

Jews, Gentiles, Church, 1 Corinthians 10:32.

Notes from the Margins of H.A.I.'s Bible

Old Testament -- Genesis – Deuteronomy

Old Testament

Genesis	25	Ecclesiastes	80
Exodus	30	Song of Solomon	83
Leviticus	35	Isaiah	85
Numbers	37	Jeremiah	91
Deuteronomy	40	Lamentations	102
Joshua	42	Ezekiel	103
Judges	43	Daniel	113
Ruth	46	Hosea	118
I Samuel	47	Joel	119
II Samuel	49	Amos	121
I Kings	5i	Obadiah	122
II Kings	54	Jonah	122
I Chronicles	57	Micah	122
II Chronicles	58	Nahum	124
Ezra	61	Habakkuk	125
Nehemiah	62	Zephaniah	126
Esther	64	Haggai	126

Job	65	Zechariah	127
Psalms	69	Malachi	128
Proverbs	75		

Genesis

The Book of Beginnings.

The seed plot of the Bible. Every doctrine afterward unfolded found in germ in this Book. Tells of Generation, Degeneration, and Regeneration. Note: Creation is distinguished from making. Creation is threefold. God created—matter v. i, life (soul) v. 20, 21, man (spirit) v. 27. No way to pass from one to the other.

1:1 The original creation—which was perfect but fell into chaos.

1:11 *After his kind*—in both vegetable and animal worlds. No room for so-called evolution.

1:26 Image is representation. *Likeness* is character.

1:27 Man not evolved from lower forms, but a special creation.

2:10 The river of Eden. Compare with the river of Rev.

22. When God rests a river flows!

3:1 Questioning the Word of God.

3:3 Adding to the Word of God.

3:4 Denying the Word of God.

3:6 Disobeying the Word of God. Lust of the flesh, lust of the eyes, pride of life.

3:9 The first question of the Old Testament. See Matt. 2.2.

4:3-4 The only two religions.

4:20-22 Note how the arts and sciences and commercial life all began in Cain's family.

5:2 Note—The mother of the race is given three names: *Adam*— Headship of the man recognized. She is seen in him. *Isha*— Woman. Her place in nature. *Eve*— Living. The name given her by faith after the fall, and the promise of life.

5:21 (Methuselah) *When he dies it shall be sent,* i.e., the flood. Note that he lived up to the date of the flood.

6:11 *As it was in the days of Noah*—Corruption and violence are again to fill the earth in the time of the end, immediately before the manifestation of the Son of Man.

8:20 Dispensation of Government begins.

9:6 Capital punishment divinely instituted.

9:21-22 He was set in authority as the first ruler in the earth: failed to rule himself.

10:8-10 The Great Apostate. A hunter of the souls of men— Founder of idolatry at Babylon.

10:22 Job was of this tribe (Uz).

11:4 Beginning of Babylon. The first "skyscraper."

11:31—12:1 Note from Stephen's speech in Acts 7, that the call to Abram to go out had preceded this family emigration.

12:7 The covenant of the land has never been rescinded.

See ch. 13:14. 12:10 The testing of faith: Abraham's failure.

12:11 A sinful compact—A wrong start. See ch. 20:13.

14:4 Thirteen—the number of rebellion or disorder. 14:13-16 The separated man is the one to aid his entangled brother. First time the term Hebrew is used in Scripture.

15:6 *Believed (Amen-ed)* this is the first use of *Amen* in the Bible. Justification by faith—Rom. 4.

16:1 The expedient of the flesh.

17:4 The Covenant fully stated.

17:8 Possession of the land included in the Covenant. Ch. 24:7.

20:2 The unjudged sin of earlier days, repeated. 0:6 What mercy!

20:9 What a rebuke to a man of faith from a Philistine!

20:12 A half truth is a whole lie.

21:1 The promise fulfilled *as He had said.*

21:21 The flesh united to the world.

22:1 Tempt and test—or try, are all the same word.

22:6-8 The Father and the Son went *both of them together* to the place where Christ offered up Himself!

22:12 God spared that father's heart the pang He would not spare His own.

23:2 The death of the Mother—dispensationally the setting aside of Israel after the Cross.

24 The call of the Bride—dispensationally the Church called out. The unnamed servant typical of the Holy Spirit who speaks not from or of himself, seeking a bride in a far country for the son.

24:11-15 The bride found at the well—the water of the Word.

24:15 *While they are yet speaking, I will hear.*

24:22 The earnest of what should be hers later as the bride of the son.

24:58 The bride's decision—"purpose of heart."

25:1 Dispensationally the restoration of the earthly people—A nation born in a day.

25:5 The exalted son.

26:7 The father's failure reproduced in the son.

26:18 Going back to first principles.

27:1 His spiritual condition reflected in the physical!

27:12 More concerned about what he would seem to be than what he actually was!

27:20 What hypocrisy!

27:27-29 This is not the blessing of Abraham. See ch. 28:3-4.

28:3-4 The blessing of Abraham confirmed to Jacob apart from deceit or human scheming.

28:13-14 The covenant of the land confirmed to Jacob.

28:20 Bargaining with God. No apprehension of the grace of the Lord.

30:37-43 Fleshly scheming. Needless scheming. God's plans working out just the same.

31:29 *Thou could'st have no power at all against me, except it were given thee from heaven.*

31:40 True shepherd service.

32:20 *Appease him*—literally, "Cover his face." In such manner do sinful men—conscious of their guilt—seek to cover the face of God—so He will not see their sins.

32:24-26 The unseen wrestler—breaking down the strength of nature. When Jacob can no longer struggle, he *clings* to the One who has brought his strength to naught.

33:13-14 The true shepherd heart. See ch. 31:40.

35:2-3 A new beginning.

35:11 The Abrahamic covenant renewed to Jacob.

37:3 The father's beloved.

37:5-10 Hated for his witness to the evil deeds of his brethren after the flesh—to be exalted as head and lord in due time.

37:14 From Hebron ("Communion") to seek his wayward brethren.

37:20-28 Rejected and sold. Delivered up to death in figure.

39:7 The temptation of Joseph.

39:13-15 Joseph falsely accused.

40 The only two religions. The dream of salvation. The dream of judgment.

41:45 Zaphnath-paaneah—in Heb. "Saviour of the world."

41:55 *Go unto Joseph.* None other name.

42:11 They were not spies, but neither were they "true" men. See ch. 44:16.

42:21 Exercise of conscience at last.

42:28 "Conscience doth make cowards of us all."

42:36 [last clause] Jacob's fortunes were never brighter than at this very time!

43:9 Note the change that has been wrought in Judah—the very one who once sold Joseph.

43:18 Afraid, when grace was about to be shown them.

44:12 The cup in Benjamin's sack! The best of them under condemnation.

44:16 No longer do they say "We are true men."

45:3-4 The revelation of the rejected one as the deliverer.

47:9 A long life for self; a short life for God.

48:1 The first mention of sickness in the Bible.

48:14 The second man put first by a cross.

49:3 The firstborn after the flesh set to one side. Joseph given his place.

50:15-18 How little they trusted him—because they did not know the love of his heart!

50:25 The bones of Joseph. Ex. 13:19.

50:26 [last clause] All that this world can give at the last—and a fitting introduction to the Book of Exodus which begins with Egypt as the land of bondage and of death with judgment hanging over all. Note that Israel carried up the bones of Joseph with them when they went out to go to Canaan.

Exodus

The book of Redemption—Typically sets forth God's way of delivering His people from judgment, from the power of sin and from this present evil world—See 1 Cor. 5:7, 8; Rom. 6, et al; Gal. 1:4.

Bondage and wretchedness preceding redemption. Divisions: History, chapters 1—24; Tabernacle, chapters 25—40; with parenthesis, chapters 32—34. Redemption by blood, chapters 1—12; Redemption by power, chapters 13—18.

Ruin—chapters 1—11.
Redemption—chapters 12—19.
Responsibility—chapters 20—24.
Relationship—chapters 25—40.

Pharaoh both God and King: typical of Satan: the renegade king that knows not Jesus as Pharaoh knew not Joseph.—2 Cor. 11:14. Pharaoh, the Sun—but unable to dispel the darkness. Called in Ezek. 29:3 *the great dragon*.

1 Egypt: typical of this present evil world—a land of death, bondage, affliction, darkness, and judgment. The land of Ham—swarthy, sunburnt, darkened by the light.

2 Moses: the deliverer. Type of the Coming One: Deut. 18:18, prophet, deliverer, shepherd, mediator, lawgiver, king, meekest of men—"I am meek."

2:5 It was Providence that put Moses into the court of Pharaoh. It was faith that, later, took him out of it.

2:9 The Lord's word to each Christian parent. 1 Thess. 2:7.

2:11 Moses first attempts to deliver his people in a fleshly way.

2:12 God's way of delivering Israel was not by killing Egyptians one by one. He would make a clean break in His own way. So now He does not save by delivering from one sin after another, but by a complete settlement at once.

2:15 God allowed Moses to have all the world could give, but it was in order that he might give it up for His sake. Heb. 11:24-28.

2:19 He looked like an Egyptian—reminding us of Him who came in the likeness of sinful flesh.

3:7 Sorrows seen, heard, known.

3:14

	I AM	By Myself
		In Myself
		Through Myself
		For Myself

Only God could so speak. 20 times in John's Gospel, Jesus says *I AM*.

4:2 The rod never used for personal reasons. Christ would not use His authority merely for Himself.

4:4 The Lord in rising from the dead took back the rod: He annulled Satan's power.

4:7 The leprous hand—the clean one pledged Himself to do what was in His heart—to be made sin. The hand cleansed speaks of resurrection. See Ps. 74:11; John 17:4.

4:9 The third sign—water made blood—a sign specially for unbelievers—all judgment—no grace here. It is not now that *they may believe but if they will not believe*. Compare with Heb. 6:7, 8.

4:10-14 The backwardness of the flesh may be as great an hindrance as the forwardness of the flesh. Compare the call of Moses with the call of Jeremiah. Both were lowly men—both distrusted themselves— both made excuses—both had to learn that power belongeth unto God.

6:6-8 God's seven I will's

12 Redemption by blood, typical of salvation from the guilt and judgment of sin.

12:2 A new beginning. All the past blotted out.

12:3 A lamb.

12:4 The lamb. (Have you asked your neighbor?)

12:5 Your lamb. Note that the characteristic word here is take.

12:15 Leaven always typical of evil.

13:21 The pillar of fire and cloud typical of the Holy Spirit—ch. 14:19. The fiery pillar leads ordinarily— but here follows for protection. 14:26-28 "Sin shall not have dominion over you—not under law, but grace." Redemption by power. Romans 6—8.

16:15 The manna—typical of Christ in His humiliation. Came from heaven.

White: pure.

Sweet: precious.

On the dew: In the Spirit's power.

Lowly—on the ground.

It must be gathered, or trampled on. See John 6.

17:8 Amalek: type of the lusts of the flesh.

17:11-12 Prevailing intercession on high—type of our great Intercessor in Heaven whose hands are never heavy!

19:4 *Two wings of the great eagle.* Rev. 12:14.

20 "Some things are commanded because they are right, and other things are right because they are commanded."

20:22 The priestly privilege to draw near. See Heb. 10. Priests before the Levitical priesthood was established. See ch. 24:5.

23:10-11 The sabbatic year. It was the neglect of this that was one of the reasons for the Babylonian Captivity.

24:3 [last clause] The confidence of the flesh.

25 The materials for the tabernacle.

Gold—divine righteousness to glory.

Silver—redemption.
Brass—judgment: endurance.

Blue—heavenly.

Purple—royalty.

Scarlet—suffering—earthly splendor.

Fine linen—righteousness.

Goats' hair—sinbearing—prophetic office.

Rams' skins—consecration.

Badger skins—separation.

Shittim wood—humanity.

Oil for the light—the Holy Spirit.

Spices—fragrance of Christ.

Sweet incense—intercession.

Precious stones—divine excellences as seen in the people of God.

25:10 The Ark—Christ the meeting place between God and man—the throne of God.

26:3 Two fives—the measure of responsibility to God and man.

26:7 The tent of goats' hair. "Made in the likeness of sinful flesh."

28:12 All the people of God upon His shoulders shall bear memorial. See w. 21, 38 also.

28:34 Testimony and fruit.

29:20-21 The whole man redeemed and consecrated by blood—then anointed with oil: the Holy Spirit.

30:12-13 Redeemed by silver—Contrast 1 Pet. 1:18.

Note that when David numbered the people he omitted this—and plague followed.

32:2-4 They readily gave to the service of their false gods what they never thought of giving to Jehovah!

32:26-28 Three thousand slain: God's first dealing under law. Contrast with Pentecost!

33:15 He would far rather have God without Canaan than Canaan without God.

35:30 Bezaleel—A great-grandson of Caleb, son of Hez-ron. See 1 Chron. 2:19, 20.

37:6 What a glorious and righteous propitiatory!

38:31 The pins were not prominent but were most essential—so every member is necessary.

40:12 The washing of regeneration.

Leviticus

The Priest's Guide Book. The Book of the sanctuary—"access to God." In the New Testament there are some forty distinct references to the ordinances of Leviticus as typical.

1 The burnt offering. Christ offering Himself without spot unto God to glorify Him and on our behalf. See Ps. 40:7, 8; Eph. 5:1, 2.

2 The food offering—The perfection of Christ as Man. Christ moves through all the Gospels as the perfect meal offering.

2:4-13 Christ's introduction into this world as the place of trial and testing.

2:13 Salt: the preservative power of righteousness.

3:1 In Luke's Gospel Christ is seen as the Peace Offering.

3:16 [last clause] Superabundant energy all for God.

4 The different grades of the sin offering would seem to indicate various degrees of apprehension of the person and work of Christ according to the intelligence, responsibility, and privilege of the worshiper. In Mark's Gospel Christ is the great Sin Offering.

5:5 Definiteness in confession.

5:11-13 Differences between the sin and trespass offerings : In the sin offering u person appears who deserves judgment. In the trespass offering sins are enumerated —but the person committing them is not particularly in view. (In Matthew's Gospel Christ is the Trespass Offering.)

7:31 The breast—the love of Christ.

7:32 The shoulder—the strength of Christ.

10:14 The enjoyment of the love and strength of Christ can only be *in a clean place.*

11:3 Walk and word must be in agreement.

11:13-20 All carrion-feeders were unclean, and all birds or other creatures of the night. "Ye are children of the light."

11:30 What a lot of ferrets there are! And they generally think everyone unclean but *themselves.*

12:8 The offering of the mother of Jesus.

13:2 *Skin of his flesh.* Leprosy in the body—the lusts of the flesh are their fearful result.

13:13 [last phrase] Leprosy of the head—See vv. 43, 44.

The lusts of the mind just as evil in the sight of God as the lusts of the flesh.

13:47-48 Leprosy in the garments: that is evil in the ways or behavior. Garments speak of habits.

13:52 Destroy—or judge the evil habit.

14:1-7 Not until Christ came do we read of this law being carried out *for a testimony unto them.*

14:9 *Hair,* the strength of nature—all to be done away by the sharp razor of the Word of God.

14:25-28 It is Christ's work that saves—not my understanding of it. The weakest believer is as truly redeemed by His blood and anointed by His Spirit as is the strongest saint.

16:14 Once is enough for God. Seven times to give man a perfect standing before the throne.

21:18 *He that hath a flat nose*—lacking discernment.

22:3 Holiness required in worshipers.

23:17 *Firstfruits.* James 1:18.

24—27 The claims of God—practical holiness.

25:9-10 The jubilee to sound on the day of atonement. Liberty based on sacrifice.

25:23 The land of Palestine belongs to God.

27:16 *According to the seed*—i.e., the amount of land that could be seeded with an homer of grain.

Numbers

The Levites' Guide Book. The Book of experience—of testing—and therefore of failure on man's part. The Wilderness Book.

2:2, 3 God's well-ordered camp. The Tabernacle "in the midst."—Type of Christ: "The Word became flesh and tabernacled among us."—Jesus in the midst.

3:9 Ministry waiting on priesthood. Service waiting on worship.

3:48-51 Redeemed with silver—Contrast 1 Peter 1:18.

7 Each aspect of the work of the Cross represented in the offering of each prince.

8:11-12 The Levites "a living sacrifice"—Romans 12:1.

Wholly devoted to the service of God and to the house of the Lord.

8:19 Ministry to wait upon worship.

8:21 See Rom. 12:2.

9:18 Guidance—Ps. 25:15; Isa. 11:3.

10:2 Two trumpets the two Testaments.

10:31 With the cloud to lead!

10:33 No need of Hobab's keenness and knowledge of the wilderness.

11:7 Manna: typical of Christ in humiliation.

13:26 *The firstfruits of the Spirit*—Rom. 8.

14:22 Ten temptations:

> 1. Ex. 5:20-23
> 2. Ex. 14:11-12
> 3. Ex. 15:23-25
> 4. Ex. 16:1-3
> 5. Ex. 17:1-5
> 6. Ex. 32:1-8
> 7. Num. 11:1-3
> 8. Num. 11:4-io
> 9. Num. 12:1-8; Deut. 1:22
> 10. Num. 13, 14

14:40 The energy of the flesh.

14:44 Presumption is not faith.

15:2 God's promise fulfilled despite all the faithlessness on their part.

15:5) 7 The drink offering—"He poured out His soul unto death."

15:38 The ribbon of blue. See Deut. 22:12. The heavenly color. A people linked with the God of Heaven. In type: the heavenly calling.

16:1 Note the psalms "for the sons of Korah." This man's descendants were part of the choir of the sanctuary in after days.

16:13 Rejection of the divinely appointed prince.

17:5-7 Dry rods in which was no life—typical of men in their natural estate.

17:8 The Dead One that came to life—the resurrection priesthood.

19:6 Cedar—man at his best. Hyssop—man at his worst. Scarlet—the glory of the world. All gone for faith in the death of Christ. Gal. 6:14.

19:9 *Ashes—It is finished.*

19:21 It is defiling to have to do with evil—even in seeking to deliver another. See Jude 23.

20:14 Edom—typical of the flesh. No short cut through Edom to the land of rest.

21:8-9 The brazen serpent and the springing Well. Connect with John ch. 3-4. A serpent—Christ made sin. But no poison in it—harmless—yet "like" the serpents that bit the people.

24:24 A prophecy that links with Daniel's great prophecies of the Times of the Gentiles.

29 Does the descending scale of offerings imply that piety will decline in the millennium?

31:49, 50 A voluntary offering as an expression of the gratitude of their hearts.

Deuteronomy

The Book of Review.—The Second Law.

1:19 *Kadesh-barnea*—the place of opportunity.

1:22 The sending of the spies originated in the will and unbelief of the people.

2:14 Thirty-eight years of wandering in the wilderness because of unbelief.

4:9 "Forgetful Green" in *Pilgrim's Progress*—See v. 23.

6:23 Brought out to be brought in.

10:3-4 The handwriting of ordinances—Col. 2:14.

14:12-19 All birds of the night were unclean—"Ye are not of the night nor of the darkness." All birds of prey unclean.

17:15-17 Note that Solomon gave no heed to these commands, but did all that is here forbidden.

18:10 Spiritism forbidden.

18:15 Fulfilled in Christ the True Prophet.

20:8 Note how this was carried out in the case of Gideon's army—Judges 7:3.

20:12 *Preaching peace by Jesus Christ.* If peace is refused—then judgment.

21:3 Jerusalem, the guilty city, where "also our Lord was crucified."

21:16 Firstborn not necessarily the one born first. See Ps. 89:27. A title of dignity.

21:18 The Old Testament prodigal—Contrast with Luke 15.

23:9 Holiness essential to victory.

24:1-2 Contrast the command of the Lord in Matt. 19— See also 1 Cor. 7, et al.

24:4 Yet such is the grace of God toward Israel, His divorced wife, that He will take her again when she repents of her sin. See the Book of Hosea, and Jer.

27:5 See Elijah at Carmel.

28:23-24 Brass and iron both typical of judgment and endurance. See v. 48.

28:49 [last clause], 50 Prophetic description of the Romans and the destruction of Jerusalem and its results.

28:51-56 See all this confirmed in the desolation of Palestine following the siege under Titus, etc. 28:68 [last clause] The slave markets of the world glutted with Jewish slaves.

31:3 [last clause] Joshua—type of Christ Risen who leads the people into their inheritance. 31:29 Compare Paul's last address to the elders of Ephesus.

32:8 Israel—the center of all God's thoughts for the earth.

33:2, 3 The Appearing of Jehovah on Sinai—similar to the Appearing of Christ with all His saints. God's people in His heart, in His hand, at His feet. See v. 12.

33:24 "He who dips his foot in oil leaves a mark behind" —the walk in the Spirit.

[Throughout Deuteronomy Dr. Ironside has underscored the word *remember*, and written it again and again in the margin. It is striking how often this word occurs.]

Old Testament -- Joshua - 2 Chronicles

Joshua

Entering into the inheritance.

Connect with the Epistle to the Ephesians.

3 The Ark, typical of Christ, must go down into the river of judgment to turn back the waters from the people.

3:16-17 Clear back to the first man Adam. The backward and forward aspects of the work of the Cross.

4:8 Risen with Christ, in figure.

4:9 Death with Christ, in figure.

4:20 Gilgal, the place of self-judgment—See ch. 5:2.

5:2 Sharp knives to be used on the flesh before beginning the conquest of the land.

5:11-12 Old Corn—Christ in Resurrection. Manna—Christ in humiliation—food for the wilderness.

6:18 Jericho: the city of the curse.

6:25 Rahab became an ancestress of the Messiah. See Matt. 1:5.

7:3, 4 The confidence of the flesh leading to defeat. 9:4 "The wiles of the devil."

10:1 *Adoni-zedec*—Lord of Righteousness. In type, the Satanic kingdom arrayed against the people of God— as in Eph. 6.

10:24, 25 "The God of peace shall bruise Satan under your feet shortly."

10:43 Back to Gilgal—The place of circumcision—i.e., of self-judgment.

13 The Philistines of Egyptian origin—yet giving their name to all the land "Palestine" or Philistia. "Natural man intruding into and dominating spiritual things."

15:8 The border of "praise" so close to "Gehenna"!

17:3, 4 The energy of faith in these women gave them an inheritance among their brethren.

20 Christ is the true city of refuge.

20:3 "Through ignorance ye did it." "Ye who have fled for refuge."

20:7 First mention of Galilee—See ch. 21:32.

"The name of the Lord is a strong tower. The righteous runneth into it and is safe."

21:18 Anathoth—the city of Jeremiah. Jer. 1:1.

22:4 If Joshua had given them rest! See Heb. 3—4.

22:12 Needless alarm—hasty judgment.

22:16 Unjust accusation.

22:22 The soft answer that turned away wrath.

22:30 The people pacified.

24:15 The Great Divide. Choose ye! Today it is a choice between:
1—A Saviour and a destroyer.
2—Two Masters.
3—Two lives.
4—Two deaths—"In the Lord" or "In your sins."
5—Two resurrections.
6—Two judgments.
7—Two destinies.

24:32 The bones of Joseph—See Heb. 11.

Judges

1:26 One Canaanite spared builds another Luz.

1:29 [last clause] An element of weakness left.

2:10 It is thus that every divine movement has failed eventually.

3:8 First servitude. Chushan-rishathaim—blackness of double wickedness.

3:9 Othniel—first judge.

3:12 Second servitude.

3:15-16 Ehud—the second judge. The left hand is the hand of weakness— "when I am weak then am I strong."

3:31 Shamgar—the third judge.

4:1 Third servitude.

4:4 Deborah—fourth judge.

4:21 Slain with the nail of the pilgrim's tent!

5:11 *rehearse*—Same word as "lament" in ch. 11:40. See margin of that text.

5:12 Captivity captive, i.e., lead captive your captors. See Isa. 14:2.

6:1 Fourth servitude.

6:11 Gideon, the fifth judge. Threshing out the wheat in secret— picture of a man who values the food God has provided and searches out the truth when alone with God.

6:13 Why?

6:14 The irresistible might of weakness.

6:36-40 A dispensational picture. The dew of the Spirit

on Israel. Israel forsaken—the Spirit sanctifies the nations.

7:5-7 Only those who did not stop to satisfy natural craving were fit for God's work.

7:20 Broken vessels that the light may shine out. 2 Cor. 4.

8:18 [last part] Rom. 8:29.

8:23 Gideon free from one ambition is snared by another!

9:9 The olive—Israel in covenant relationship.

9:11 The fig tree—Israel nationally.

9:13 The vine—Israel spiritually.

9:15 The bramble—Reigning—typical of antichrist Israel in apostasy.

10:1 Tola, the sixth judge.

10:3 Jair, the seventh judge.

10:6 Fifth servitude.

11:1 Jephthah, the eighth judge.

11:40 *Lament*—to talk with.

12:6 And this between brethren!

12:8 Ibzan, the ninth judge.

12:11 Elon, the tenth judge.

12:13 Abdon, the eleventh judge.

13:1 Sixth servitude. The Philistines of Egyptian origin "natural men intruding into spiritual things and bringing the people of God into bondage."

13:18 His Name shall be called "Wonderful." Isa. 9:6.

13:24 Samson the twelfth judge.

14 God using a man to fulfill His own purposes, in spite of himself. Samson was continually getting in God's way yet He wrought through him in power.

15:16 Literally: "With the jaw bone of an ass I made asses of them."

16 The defiled Nazarite rendered powerless and made captive by the world.

16:19 Sleeping in the lap of the world.

17:9 The hireling in search of a paying position.

18:19-20 A call to a larger sphere of usefulness.

18:30 Manasseh—Moses. The N inserted—a forgery.

19:22 The sin of Sodom found among the people of the covenant.

20:16 *lefthanded*—"When I am weak, then am I strong."

21 A carnal expedient to overcome the effects of an ill-considered vow. Cruelty follows rashness.

Ruth

The Kinsman-Redeemer

1 Decision for Christ.

1:2 Moab—the land of easy-going profession. Moab related to Israel through Lot. 1:5 Moab proves to be just a graveyard. 1:9 No rest in Moab.

2 Meeting with Christ.

2:7-10 The gleanings were for the poor and the stranger. Note how Ruth takes the place where grace can meet her.

3 Rest in Christ.

3:4 Trust in the integrity of Boaz.

3:7 Seeking rest at the feet of Boaz.

3:12, 13 The nearer kinsman: the first covenant to whom was given the first opportunity to redeem.

4 Union with Christ.

4:1 The claims of the nearer kinsman. The law must be met first!

4:2 The ten elders like the ten commandments were but witness of the inability of the law to redeem a stranger and an outcast

4:8 [last clause] "It is finished."

4:9 The claims of law fully met.

1 Samuel

4:5, 6 An empty sound! A false confidence.

4:7 A needless fear.

5:3 The false confronted with the true.

5:9 Apparently the Bubonic plague.

6:12 God meeting ignorant but honest people on their own ground.

7:9 *sucking lamb*—The expression of utmost feebleness.

8 Neither grace nor gift are inherited.

9:1-3 "Saul went out to seek his father's asses, and he found a nation of them ready to make him king"— D. L. Moody.

9:9 Evidently inserted by the Holy Spirit's direction in later times.

9:17 *Behold the man*—Ecco Homo!

10:1 [at end of verse] There is an omission here in the Hebrew text supplied in the Vulgate: "And thou shalt deliver His people out of the hands of their enemies, which are round about them. And this token shalt thou have that the Lord hath anointed thee to be prince."

12:11 Bedan—supposed to be Samson.

13:12-13 The activity of the flesh that could not wait God's time.

14:1 The energy of faith that confers not with flesh and blood.

14:2 The slothfulness of the flesh.

14:3 *Ichabod's brother*—i.e., one like unto him who mourns departed glory but does nothing to retrieve the circumstances.

14:6 Counting on God.

14:7 Fellowship in service.

14:13 Faith that will not be balked by difficulties.

14:24 Legal restrictions that were quite unnecessary.

14:25-29 *Honey*: the sweetness of natural things—to be used in moderation but forbidden by the legalist. Jonathan takes the honey on the end of the pilgrim's rod and is strengthened thereby.

14:32 Self-indulgence the result of legal asceticism—See Col. 3. License the fruit of legality.

14:41 [after Israel] There is an omission here in the Hebrew text, owing to a scribe's blunder: "Lord God, give Thou judgment why it is that Thou answerest me not today. If this iniquity be in me, or in Jonathan my son, give Urim; or if this iniquity be in Thy people Israel, give Thummim."

17:51 Destroyed him that had the power of death.

18:1 Jonathan's heart won for David who had taken his place and slain him that had the power of death.

18:4 Jonathan strips himself for David. Compare with Paul in Phil. 3, "What things were gain to me, those I counted loss for Christ." See ch. 19:2.

19:2-7 Jonathan loyal to David. He "speaks well of David"—confession and defense. See ch. 20:1.

20:33 Sharing David's shame.

21:13 What a condition and position for a man of faith!

22:1 The rejected one as the center of gathering. Jonathan not seen in this company, but see ch. 23:16.

23:16 Jonathan's last visit with David. He returns to his "high places" while David is in rejection.

24:6 Saul is recognized by David as Messiah of Jehovah! He was still the Lord's Anointed.

25:9 Compare "in My Name" in John 14-16.

27:1 Yet God was caring for David in a marvelous way at this very time.

27:10 What a position for the man after God's own heart to occupy!

29 What a position for the anointed king of Israel! The result of unbelief.

30:13 Egypt: the world. Amalek: the lusts of the flesh.

30:21 "Good news" or "cold water." "As good news from a far country."

2 Samuel

1:8 Saul spared some of Amalek and suffered indignity at the hands of an Amalekite at the end.

1:25-26 Jonathan lacked "one thing." He loved David but he did not fully share his rejection.

2:10 Already a breach between Israel and David.

4:4 Mephibosheth—lame by a fall!

5:8 *soul*—seat of the emotions.

7:1 5 The thoughts of God are often different to those of the best of His servants.

7:19 "The sure mercies of David."

42

7:25 Faith says "Amen" to God's promise.

8:11 David does not take the glory to himself, but dedicates the gifts to God.

9 A gospel picture. The kindness of God shown to the fallen sons of Adam.

10:3-4 David's kindness spurned, his ambassadors put to shame.

11:1, 2 Slothfulness preceded David's fearful fall.

11:8 Attempting to cover up his sin.

11:9 Uriah's devotedness.

12:5 Easy to become indignant over the supposed wrongdoing of another while covering one's own sin!

12:11 Governmental consequences that confession could not turn aside.

13 The awful effects of David's sin manifested in his own household.

13:31 Bitter reaping.

15:7 *After forty years*—i.e., after he was forty years old.

Rank hypocrisy!

16:3 Misrepresentation of Mephibosheth's motives.

16:6-8 God himself said that David was a man of blood—but it was in righteousness. See 1 Chron. 22:8.

17 Ahithophel's opportunity for revenge. He was the grandfather of Bath-sheba. See 1 Chron. 3:5—and connect with 2 Sam. 15:12.

17:23 Prototype of Judas, the son of perdition.

17:27 *Machir*. He who had protected Mephibosheth is now loyal to David.

18:22 Running unsent.

19:9-15 BRINGING BACK THE KING! In the king's absence confusion reigns. While God's Anointed is rejected man's efforts to put things to rights are doomed to failure. We see this today in the world which needs a competent ruler. Connect with the parable of the rejected kingdom in Luke 19:12.

19:14 The king awaits the invitation of all his own to return.

19:37 Tradition says that Chimham was the owner of the inn at Bethlehem, where hundreds of years later the Lord was born. See 1 Kings 2:7; Jer. 41:17.

20:9 A Judas kiss. Amasa was Joab's cousin (ch. 17:25), probably illegitimate. 1 Chron. 2:16.

23:8-39 The honor roll. Joab not in the list.

23:39 Uriah honored by God though cruelly wronged by David.

24:3 A carnal man shows more good sense than the man after God's own heart.

1 Kings

A period of 108 years (Usher) B.C. 1015-897. In Kings man attempts to rule and is ever a failure. In Chronicles God overrules all in view of Messiah's Kingdom.

1:6 [first part] No wonder he became a rebel!

2:12—11:43 Reign of Solomon. 2:34 Joab's inglorious end.

3:1 Typical of the Gentiles being blessed in the latter day. Isa. 19:21-25.

3:6-9 Solomon's prayer. 3:11-14 God's answer. 3:16-28 Solomon's discernment.

4:31 Solomon's wisdom. He knew more than all men of the orbits of the planets, of the origination of light and fixed sustaining systems and the results of the revolving spheres.

4:33 The cedar symbolic of man at his best; the hyssop, man in his lowest estate. See Ex. 12:22.

5:1-5 Kings opens with the Temple built and closes with the Temple burnt.

6:1 i.e., after deducting the years of servitude to their enemies.

6:7 The building rising in silence.

7:10 "Built upon the foundation of the apostles and prophets."

7:25 The universality of the Word of the truth of the gospel. "Into all the world."

8:3-8 That which was but temporary and for the wilderness merged into what was settled and in the land. The only piece of furniture that belonged to the Tabernacle which was not replaced in the Temple by a new piece. No need for staves now: the Ark at rest at last.

8:10-11 The cloud of glory—typical of the Holy Spirit— taking possession of the material Temple—as the Spirit took possession of the spiritual temple in Acts 2.

8:18 Comforting assurance.

10:13 Exceeding abundantly above all we ask or think.

10:14 666 the number of a man—Rev. 13.

11 Solomon's failure.

11:1-2 What a lamentable break!

11:14 Edom—type of the flesh.

11:17 The flesh is at home in the world of which Egypt is the type.

11:19 The flesh in high favor with the God of this world.

12 The kingdom divided.
From chapter 12 on: The divided kingdom—never to be one again till Jesus reigns.

12:6 Rehoboam—a weak man who pretends to strength he does not possess.

12:20 Jeroboam—first king of Israel. 19 kings of Israel.

13 The disobedient prophet.

13:11 Satan's wiles. Another prophet succeeds where a king failed.

13:18 The word of an angel against the Word of God.

14:21 *Rehoboam*—king of Judah (1)

14:24 Nothing too low for people away from God.

14:27 Imitation to keep up appearances.

15:1 *Abijah* or *Abijam*—king of Judah (2).

15:8 *Asa*—king of Judah (3).

15:25 *Nadab*—king of Israel (2).

15:27 *Baasha*—a second dynasty. King of Israel (3).

16:6 *Elah*—king of Israel (4).

16:10 *Zimri*—a third dynasty. King of Israel (5).

16:15 The shortest reigns of any of the kings.

16:23 *Omri*—king of Israel (6). Fourth dynasty.

16:24 *Samaria*—Omri's capital is called, on the Assyrian monuments, Beth Omri.
Omri introduced Baal worship into Israel in a legal way —and Ahab "carried on." See Mic. 6:16.

16:29 *Ahab*—king of Israel (7).

16:31 "That woman Jezebel." Connect with Rev. 2— Thyatira.

18:24 Baal was the sun god—the god of fire.

18:31 *twelve stones*—unity still recognized.

20:22 Preparedness. "In time of peace, prepare for war."

20:32 What a blunder!

20:39-40 A lesson in personal work and responsibility—busy here and there!

22:4 Jehoshaphat the man who could not say "no"! The unequal yoke.

22:7 An uneasy conscience.

22:15 Ironical speech.

22:41 *Jehoshaphat*—king of Judah (4).

22:51 *Ahaziah*—king of Israel (8).

2 Kings

Covers a period of 308 years B.C. 896-588 (Usher)

Continues the history of the divided kingdom.

2 Rapture of Elijah. Elisha's ministry covers chapters 2—13.

2:1, 2 Gilgal—rolling. Where the reproach of Egypt was rolled away: the place of self-judgment. Beth-el: the house of God.

2:4 Jericho: the city of palm trees—but under the curse. This present evil world.

2:6 Jordan: the river of judgment.

2:9 [last clause] A double portion. Note: Elisha wrought twice as many miracles as Elijah.

3:1 *Jehoram*—king of Israel (9).

3:7 Jehoshaphat enters again into an unequal yoke.

3:16 Lower down.

4:2, 3 The oil of grace must be appropriated to be multiplied.

4:6 As long as there is one vessel to receive it, the supply of the Spirit will not be exhausted.

4:10 Rest, communion, discipleship, instruction.

4:31 The prophet's staff worthless in the hands of a carnal man.

5:2 A little missionary.

5:22 The lying plea of a covetous man.

5:23 The glad gift of a grateful heart.

5:27 Divine retribution. See ch. 8:4.

7:1 God's salvation and the scorner's doom.

7:3 Salvation for the worst—not only starving but unclean.

7:12 Unbelief.

8:4, 5 Gehazi telling of Elisha's deeds while suffering himself because of his own failure and sin.

8:16 *Jehoram*—king of Judah (5).

8:26 *Ahaziah*—king of Judah (6).

9 *Jehu*—king of Israel (10).

9:28 Ahaziah's bad end because of the company he kept.

10:22 Only place where we read of a "vestry" in the Bible.

10:35 *Jehoahaz*—king of Israel (10).

11:2 Joash "the hidden king."

11:3 *Athaliah*—ruler of Judah (7).

12:1 *Jehoash*—king of Judah (8).

12:9 The chest beside the altar.

13:4 Jehoahaz—the only king of Israel who is ever said to have sought the Lord.

13:10 *Jehoash*—king of Israel (12).

13:14-20 Last scenes in the life of Elisha.

14:1 *Amaziah*—king of Judah (9).

14:6 The Pentateuch cited in the days of Amaziah.

14:21 *Azariah* or *Uzziah*—king of Judah (10).

14:23 *Jeroboam* II—king of Israel (13).

15:8 *Zachariah*—king of Israel (14).

15:13 *Shallum*—king of Israel (15).

15:17 *Menahem*—king of Israel (16).

15:23 *Pekahiah*—king of Israel (17).

15:27 *Pekah*—king of Israel (18).

15:29 *Hoshea*—king of Israel (19).

15:32 *Jotham*—king of Judah (11).

16:1 *Ahaz*—king of Judah (12).

16:6 First use of the term, "the Jews."

16:14 God's altar set to one side for that of man's designing.

17:24 Origin of the Samaritans.

18:1 Hezekiah—the godly king of Judah (13). Hezekiah the Reformer, chapters 18—20.

18:3 A complete reformation. 18:4 Nehushtan!

18:13 The Assyrians attempt to do with Judah as with Israel. But God protects Judah because of Hezekiah's piety, even though weakness led him to pay tribute for a time.

21:1 Manasseh—king of Judah (14).

21:18 Amon—king of Judah (15).

22:1 Josiah—king of Judah (16).

22—23:30 Josiah the king who honored God's Word.

23:24 Spiritism, an abomination to the Lord.

23:31 Jehoahaz—king of Judah (17).

23:34 Jehoiakim—king of Judah (18).

24:8 Jehoiachin—king of Judah (19).

24:17 *Zedekiah*—king of Judah (20). Zedekiah not in the direct line. The throne rights were not his. Younger brother of Jehoahaz.

25:26 Back to the lands from which they came out, Chaldea and Egypt.

25:28 The pledge and earnest of future deliverance and restoration, according to the Word of the Lord.

1 Chronicles

Preparation for the coming King

1:10 Nimrod—the great apostate.

1:12 The Philistines of Egyptian origin—yet "in the land" "natural men intruding into spiritual things."

2:7 What a title to bear forever!

2:16 David, uncle to Joab and his brothers.

2:19 Caleb—son of Hezron, ancestor of Bethlehem. See Ex. 35:30.

3:5 Bath-sheba, mother both of Solomon and Nathan— the two lines of descent in Matt. 1 and Luke 3.

4:4 Bethlehem named for the grandson of Caleb. See ch. 2:19-20.

5:1 The one born first set aside. Joseph becomes the firstborn.

6:22 Sons of Korah.

6:31-32 Note: the sons of Korah led the choir of the sanctuary after David brought the Ark to Jerusalem. See Psalm 84.

11:13-14 Not the same incident as recorded in 2 Samuel 23.

12:15 Men of energy—not men who followed the line of least resistance.

15:21 harps on the Sheminith—i.e., "on the octave."

16:8-22 Ps. 105.

16:23-33 Ps. 96.

16:34-36 Ps. 106.

17:4 The thoughts of God are above the thoughts of His best servants.

17:23-24 Faith's Amen to God's Word. Asking according to the will of God.

18:13 Edom—typical of the flesh: held in subjection during these years of blessing.

20:1 David's sin with Bath-sheba is here passed over. His repentance accepted, it is omitted from the review.

22:2 The stones "prepared afore" for their place in the Temple.

22:6-19 David's revelation to Solomon of the coming glory. See Rev. 1:1-3.

24:7-18 Twenty-four elders or chief priests—key to Rev. 4—5. All the priesthood represented in the 24.

25:7 Twenty-four harpers. In Rev. the priests and harpers are one. Worship and praise go together.

26:10 The one born first set aside and Simri becomes the firstborn in title. See Christ in Col. 1.

28:18 See Ezek. 1, "The chariot of the cherubims."

2 Chronicles

The Preparation For The Coming King. The need of a competent ruler demonstrated. The preservation of the Davidic line.

3:5 No wood seen. Covered with gold.

4 All in tens. Responsibility fully met in the Cross.

4:2 Atonement. The Word of God for practical cleansing.

4:3 The Word of truth of the gospel.

4:4 The universality of the gospel message.

4:6 Cleansing.

4:7 Light.

4:8 Sustenance.

4:17 In the place of death.

5:9 The Ark at rest.

6:4 God's hand and mouth ever in holy agreement.

6:8 God takes note of the purpose of the heart.

10:7-11 Rehoboam's greatest blunder was in not asking counsel of the Lord before consulting with men at all.

He did not know God for himself.

10:16 Rebellion of the ten tribes.

12:10 Trying to keep up appearances.

12:14 Contrast with Ezra 7:10: "The preparation of the heart is of the Lord."

14:6 Years of obedience to, and dependence upon God.

16:9 [last clause] Wars because of failure to heed the Word of God. See ch. 15:19.

17—20 Reign of Jehoshaphat. A godly man who became entangled in unequal yoke through excessive amiability.

18:1 Increased wealth leads to an unequal yoke.

20:7-9 Reminding God of that which He would never forget. Faith taking hold of the Word.

20:19 The sons of Korah.

20:21 The singers in the van! "The joy of the Lord is your strength."

20:3 5 Jehoshaphat's one weak point. A man who could not say "No."

21:6 Fruit of the unequal yoke.

21:17 Divine retribution.

21:20 *departed without being desired*—What an epitaph!

22:11 The hidden king. All the messianic promises hung on that baby boy who was hid in the Temple.

24:8 The chest of Joash.

24:10 Hilarious, or cheerful giving. 2 Cor. 9:7.

24:20-21 Zechariah, the priest, slain "between the porch and the altar."

25:13 Suffering as a result of an unequal yoke—even though repented of.

26:5 Another Zechariah who was a prophet. See ch. 24:20; Zech. 1:1; Matt. 23:35. 26:15 [last clause] His strength became the occasion of his weakness.

26:19 Leprosy of the head. See Lev. 13.

26:20-21 The lusts of the mind. The hatefulness and uncleanness of pride manifested.

29:1-2 What a mother she must have been to rear so godly a son of so ungodly a father!

29:3 Beginning at the house of God. 29:16-17 Cleansing from within outward. Not the porch first!

29:24 [last part] The division of the kingdom not recognized. *All* Israel one people in God's eyes.

33:1-2 The ungodly son of a godly father born in the fifteen added years of his father's life.

33:12-13 Manasseh's repentance and conversion.

34:9 Many from the ten tribes linked with the tribes of Judah and Benjamin.

35:22 *Megiddo*—Armageddon.

36:21 70 sabbatic years—a cycle of 490 years in which the Word of God had been neglected as to this.

Ezra

1—2 The return of the remnant.

1:7-11 Separating the vessels to honor from the vessels to dishonor. 2 Tim. 2.

2:28 Where Abraham built his altar and pitched his tent so long before.

2:59 Uncertain as to their pedigree.

2:62 Certainty required.

3 The work of rebuilding begun.

3:3 The altar first!

3:6 The house of God next.

3:11-12 Young men are enthusiastic for the present and future. Aged men are apt to be retrospective.

4 Opposition from the enemy.

4:2 The enemy attempts to hinder—offer of amalgamation.

4:4 Weakening the hands.

4:5 Hiring counsellors against them.

4:8-10 Opposition of the heterodox "societies" to the building of the Temple to the Lord alone.

4:12 Misrepresentation. They were building the Temple.

4:23 Stopping the work by force.

5—6 The work resumed.

5:1 The Books of Haggai and Zechariah come in here.

5:5 A second letter that proved a boomerang.

5:17 *All* Israel—even though so many scattered.

7—8 Ezra's return.

7:10 Note the character of Ezra's preparation. Contrast with King Rehoboam. 2 Chron. 12:14.

8:21-22 Contrast Neh. 2:9. 8:29 "That good deposit keep."

8:33 The treasure weighed at the end of the journey, nothing lost on the way.

9—10 Ezra's ministry.

9:1 In the right position but a wrong condition.

9:5 Ezra's prayer. Compare with Neh. 9 and Dan. 9.

10:2 *Shechaniah*—this man had to join in putting away his own mother or stepmother—see v. 26.

10:26 *Jehiel*—father of Shechaniah of v. 2.

Nehemiah

An Exercised Man—Building the wall-Separation maintained.

1 Jerusalem's needy condition. Nehemiah's call.

1:11 The great king is but "this man" before God.

2 Nehemiah's commission to restore and build the city. "The failed testimony."

2:1 in the month Nisan—generally reckoned as Passover season B.C. 446, when the "command went forth to restore and build Jerusalem."

2:12 Conferring not with flesh and blood.

2:19 Opposition on the part of the enemy. (1) Ridicule.

3 Building of the wall.

The gates of Jerusalem—note that both the gate of Ephraim and prison gate are not mentioned here. Ch. 12:39.

3:1 The sheep gate. *tower of Hananeel*—a marked spot to be rediscovered in the last days. See Jer. 31:38; Zech. 14:10.

3:3 The fish gate.

3:6 The old gate. Through this the old way entered. See Jer. 6:16.

3:13 The valley gate.

3:14 The dung gate.

3:15 Gate of the fountain.

3:25 *The court of the prison*—discipline must be maintained.

3:26 The water gate.

3:28 The horse gate.

3:29 The east gate.

3:30 *over against his chamber*—evidently a lonely man in a room.

3:31 The gate Miphkad—decisions.

4:1-2 Opposition. (2) Mockery, intimidation.

4:7-8 Opposition. (3) Open warfare.

5:1 Opposition. (4) Internal dissension.

5:14 Compare with Paul who labored for his support rather than use his right as an apostle.

5:16 No real estate deals.

6 Plots and snares.

6:2 Opposition. (5) Plotting and slander.

6:10 Opposition. (6) Attempts at intimidation.

7 Restoring order.

7:64-65 "The Lord knoweth them that are His."

8 The great Bible reading.

8:4 Only place the word "pulpit" is found in the English Bible.

8:17-18 Unobserved for 1,000 years, still it was in the Book.

9 The Word and prayer.

Note—Three ninth chapters are devoted to confession:

Ezra 9—Daniel 9—Nehemiah 9.

9:3 The Word to judge their ways. Result—confession.

9:20 The Holy Spirit in the wilderness.

9:30 The Holy Spirit speaking through the prophets—2 Pet. 1:21.

10 A new start.

11 A willing people.

12 Dedication of the wall.

12:11 Jaddua—the high priest in the days of Alexander the Great.

12:39 Gate of Ephraim and the prison gate.

13 Vigilance vs. declension.

13:4 An unequal yoke— "what agreement hath the temple of God with idols?"

Esther

The Book of Providence—God's secret care over Israel. See Isa. 45:15. Where do we find Esther in the law? "I will hide myself."

The name of God not found in this Book. 1 The royal feast and the divorce of Vashti.

2 The choice of Esther.

2:18 See the "according to's" of Ephesians.

3 The wrath of the Amalekite and the letter of doom.

4 In sackcloth and ashes.

4:3 [last part] Symbols of repentance.

4:4 A change of habits will not deliver from the sentence of condemnation.

4:16 No mention of prayer as the name of God is omitted.

5 The scepter of grace—The banquet and the gallows.

6 A sleepless night and its results.

6:6 Pride goeth before destruction.

7 The second banquet and the Amalekite's end.

8 The despised man exalted and the decree of grace.

8:9 The post of mercy.

8:14 Hastened on their way with the good news!

9:1-19 The deliverance.

9:20-32 The institution of Purim.

10 Speaking peace.

Job

"A righteous man learning his own nothingness" S.R. The Book of Repentance. Also the mystery of suffering.

1—2 Historical prologue.

The testing of Job by Satan.

Job, an historical character. See Ezek. 14:14, 20; Jas.

3—41 The drama. Job's contention with his friends and the Lord's answer.

4:7 Note the philosophy of Eliphaz: the righteous are preserved from disaster. Such only comes upon the wicked!

4:17 i.e., Men punish evildoers—so with God.

5:17-18 All very true but not applicable to Job in these circumstances.

6:22-23 Job asked no favor of them.

9:2 Answered in the Epistle to the Romans.

9:9 Astronomy known to Job. Ch. 26:13; 38:31, 32.

9:13-15 Job would not have the presumption to plead his righteousness, as merit—but he feels God should shew mercy when he is not consciously guilty of any wilful sin.

9:22 For a moment Job falls back on a hard fatalistic philosophy, but he cannot rest in this.

9:29 i.e., Why should I care to justify myself, if I am a wicked, godless man?

10:22 Description of Sheol as Job understood it. 11 Zophar, the stern legalist. "So much sin, so much suffering."

11:3 lies—"sophistries."

11:3-4 "If God be for us, who can be against us?"

11:14-17 Zophar's philosophy is very simple: be good and God will bless with all temporal mercies.

12:6 It is not always the good who have temporal prosperity.

12:14 Rev. 3:7.

13:7 A Welsh collier was wont to say to his Bible class as they reasoned about the Scriptures: "Be careful, lads, that you keep the character of God clear."

13:15 Trust in God coupled with self-righteousness.

15:20 This is often true of the godly also.

21:7 The wicked not invariably recompensed in this life.

21:13 "In a moment." See 1 Cor. 15:52.

22:15-16 The Antediluvians.

23:10 Confidence where he cannot understand. A sense of moral integrity.

24:12 Many who are guilty of the very offences charged against Job yet seem to be prospered by God.

27:13-23 Job sums up all that they have declared to be the portion of the wicked—then proceeds to show that this cannot be applied to him.

28:22 The wisdom of God displayed in the Cross.

29—31 I, me, my, mine over 195 times. Job's confidence before he saw the Lord.

29:1-6 Job's former estate in the home.

29:7-10 Abroad.

29:11-17 His benevolence extolled.

29:18-20 His confidence.

29:21-25 His philanthropy.

30 Job's wretched condition at the time his friends called upon him.

30:1-8 Mocked.

30:9-12 Scorned.

30:13-15 Persecuted.

30:16-19 Suffering.

30:20-23 No answer from God.

30:24-27 Absolute misery.

30:28-31 Utter desolation.

31 Job's insistence on his own righteousness.

31:1-12 Chaste and upright.

31:13-23 Kind to all.

31:24-28 Sound in faith.

31:29-32 Friendly and hospitable.

31:33-34 Straightforward and fearless.

31:35-40 His challenge to God and man.

32 God is holy and merciful—whatever our experiences may seem to prove.

33:7-9 God's purpose in chastening vindicated.

33:13 God's ways are inscrutable.

34:12, 23 God's dealings ethically right.

34:31-32 Exercise under discipline. See Amos 7:9; Heb. 12:5.

35:7 Man makes a great mistake when he makes himself the center of things—instead of God.

35:14 Trust where you cannot trace!

36:5-12 Elihu epitomises the teaching of Job's three friends—and shows that Job himself has held the same philosophy and has actually justified himself rather than God.

36:24 "Whatever else you do keep the character of God clear!"

37:1 Thunderstorm is approaching!

37:5 This should teach us humility!

37:12 All nature under God's control—yet all inexplicable.

37:13 So with all His dealings with men.

38—41 Jehovah speaks.

A whirlwind comes across the desert and the voice of God speaks out of it. God asks Job 79 or 80 questions he cannot answer.

38:22, 23 i.e., The wars of the elements—and God has at times used these very things for the defeat or victory of armies.

38:31 Astronomy testifies to the power and wisdom of God. Ch. 9:9.

40:4, 5 Job's first answer to Jehovah's challenge. 40:8 Shall man question God's righteousness if affliction comes upon him?

42:1-6 Job's second and last answer—"The end of the Lord."

42:16 Job lived in the patriarchal age before life was shortened as now.

Psalms

Book 1 Chapters 1 to 41

Divine Principles—The Genesis Book—The Counsels of God as to Christ.

1—8 The anointed King—rejected by Israel—owned as Son of Man. Psalms 1, 2, 8 messianic.

1:5 *stand—Standing*—ability to abide divine scrutiny. See Ps. 5:5.

2:1-3 The voice of the world. 2:4-6

The voice of the Father.

2:7-9 The voice of the Son.

2:10-12 The voice of the Spirit.

9—15 Antichrist and the enemy of God—the eventual victory over the powers of evil.

16—41 Christ in the midst of Israel—God manifested.

Psalms 16, 17, 18, 21, 22, 23, 24, 40, 41 messianic. The perfect meal offering. Christ as the Dependent Man here on the earth.

16:5 my cup—See Ps. 23:5.

16:14 Dwellers on the earth. See Phil. 3.

18:17 His mighty power which He wrought in Christ when He raised Him from the dead.

19:1-6 The testimony of God's works in creation. 19:7-14 The testimony of God's Word.

22 Psalm of the Cross—the sin offering—the Good Shepherd. Christ suffering at the hands of God.

22:3 Who was praising but He, at this time of His soul's sorrow?

22:6 Tolaath—the scarlet worm.

23 Psalm of the crook—the Great Shepherd.

24 Psalm of the crown—the Chief Shepherd. 25—39 Experiences of the godly remnant.

25:5 A great salvation for men whose iniquity is great, See v. 11.

25:9 Guidance—Matt. 11:29, 30. See Hos. 11:3.

25:11 We might have said, "It is not very great!"

25:15 Guidance—Ps. 32:8; Num. 9:18-22.

27:4 One thing—See Phil 3:13. The beauty of the Lord. See Isa. 53:2. See Ps. 29:2.

29:3-5 A storm in the mountains moving on into the wilderness.

31:1 See 1 John 1:9.

32:7 Hiding in God instead of hiding from Him.

33:7 *as an heap*—"in a bottle" correct text.

34:16 Note that Peter omits the last half of this verse. 1 Pet. 3:12.

36:8 The river of God. Ezek. 47:1-12.

40 Psalm of the burnt offering.

41:9 Judas—antichrist.

Book 2 Chapters 42—72

The Fallen State of Israel—Their ruin and redemption.

Ps. 45, 55, 68, 69, 72 messianic.

42—51 The King coming to reign. The hope of the needy.

44:12 "Ye have sold yourselves for nought and shall be redeemed without money." Isa. 52:3.

45:11 Beauty. Ps. 29:2.

45:13-14 See the bride in Rev. 19.

45:17 See Luke 22:19; Jer. 16:7.

48:14 unto—"over."

49:7-9 Redemption. See Lev. 25:48. Costly—so let it alone forever. 50:3 Isa. 65:6.

50:15 A promise for him who observes v. 14.

52—60 Soul exercises leading to deliverance.

55:19 *have no changes*—"settled on the lees."

61—72 Deliverance through the Redeemer-King.

62 Note the use of the word "only."

64:6 [first clause] "Love covereth a multitude of sins."

66:18 The one great hindrance to prayer.

68:11 Feminine—a company of women.

68:30 *pieces of silver*—redemption money. See Ex. 30.

69 Psalm of the trespass offering. Christ suffering from the hands of men—result, judgment. Contrast with Ps. 22.

69:4 [last clause] Christ Himself, making up for man's wrongdoing.

71:1-2 Save in righteousness. Rom. 1:17.

72 A millennial psalm.

72:16 The remnant of Israel.

73—89 Book 3.—The Leviticus series. The sanctuary. God's holiness maintained in His ways with Israel.—Psalm 89 is messianic.

73—83 Holiness manifested in grace.

73:17 *their end.* See 1 Pet, 4:17.

73:24 Or, "after the glory, receive me."

74:5-7 Builders, or destroyers?

74:8 Synagogues in the O.T.!

75:2-3 Messiah tells how He will judge in righteousness.

75:8 "Let this cup pass!"

76:10 "Ye know what restraineth."

77:2 Hand was stretched out.

77:3 *was troubled*—"I moaned."

77:7-9 Six questions of the troubled soul.

77:10-15 Faith's answer.

78:29 Prayer answered in judgment.

78:36 Flattering God!

78:68 Zion—chosen in electing grace.

79:9 Heb. 9—10.

80:15 Christ: the Branch of the Lord—to take the place of the failed people. Isa. 11:1-2.

83 Victory over the last assault of the enemy.

84—89 Christ the Mediator maintaining the holiness of God.

84 The sons of Korah—direct descendants of Korah the apostate. Num. 16 and 26. See 1 Chron.

6:31. Saved from going down to the pit.

84:3 "God's pensioners."

85 Psalm of the peace offering.

85:6 Conditions of Revival: facing facts, confession, restitution, prayer, work, obedience.

88 Under the curse of a broken law.

89:14 The cherubim. Ps. 97:2.

89:30-32 Divine discipline following disobedience.

89:37-38 The covenant not abrogated though the house of David no longer is in evidence. See Acts 15:16.

90—106 Book 4.—The first man replaced by the Second Man. The numbers Book. Experiences of the remnant as scattered among the nations. Psalms 91, 102 messianic.

90—93 Christ linking the Creator and His creation after sin had come in.

90:17 Ps. 27:4. The beauty of the Lord. See Ps. 96:6-9.

94—100 Salvation by Judgment.

94:9 "Mine ear hast Thou digged."

95:5 *The sea*—Rev. 21:1-3; Ps. 104:25.

97:11 *gladness*—"a festival of joy."

99:8 Grace and government.

100—106 Salvation realized.

102 A Gethsemane psalm.

102:25 The Father's answer to the prayer of the Son. See Heb. 1.

103:7 Note the difference between His ways (counsels) and His acts.

104:2 The Invisible God. "The radiant light is the shadow of God."—Plato

104:15 Wine to cheer, bread to strengthen.

105:25 We might have thought the devil did it!

106:15 Prayer answered in judgment.

106:33 A provoked spirit: a wrong state because of occupation with evil.

107—150 Book 5.—The Deuteronomy section. Israel restored to God. The conclusion of His ways with men.

Psalms no, 118 messianic.

107—113 Divine principles.

107:20 Healing in the Word.

109:4 "I am prayer." It is He who is the Great Intercessor.

109:8 Spoken prophetically of Judas the traitor.

111—118 Called "the Egyptian Hall-El" or "Little Hall-El."

111:9 Only place *reverend* is found in the English Bible.

114—119 God known as the Saviour.

116:8 Threefold deliverance. 2 Cor. 1:10.

116:16 Service that springs from deliverance through redemption.

118:22 The rejected stone.

118:24 The Lord's Day.

118:26 The entry into Jerusalem.

118:27 The Cross.

119 The golden alphabet—The law written upon the heart.

119:5 *directed to*—made so direct that I might.

119:9 "The washing of water by the Word."

119:30 Blessed choice!

119:44-45 The perfect law of liberty. See Jas. 2:12.

119:63 David's denomination, v. 94.

119:67 Blessed use of affliction.

119:100 Understanding the mind of God and obedience to His Word go together.

119:108 Fruit of the lips—See Is. 57:19; Heb. 13:15.

119:160 True from Genesis. See Isa. 46:9-10; 34:16.

120—134 The psalms or songs of degrees.

135—150 Salvation celebrated. Review of God's ways.

136:26 *God of heaven*—the name used in the postcaptivity Books, Ezekiel, Nehemiah, and in Daniel.

137:7-9 Divine judgment to fall on Edom: type of the flesh—See prophecy of Obadiah. Also on Babylon. See Jer. 50, 51.

139:1-6 The divine omniscience.

139:5 "Thou art around me on all sides and Thou art holding Thy hand over me." Lit. trans.

139:7-12 The divine omnipresence.

139:13-18 The divine omnipotence active on man's behalf.

139:16 [last part] True of the mystical Body of Christ, as of the human body.

139:19-24 The Divine Judgment.

141:2 Incense—typical of prayer. See Ex. 30:34.

146—150 "The Great Hall-El."

147:4-5 He numbers the stars but His understanding cannot be numbered.

149:6 a *two-edged sword*—the Word—see Eph. 6:17 and Heb. 4:12.

Proverbs

The wisdom that created the heavens now deigns to show a safe path through the world. Note:

Throughout it is family instruction; the teaching of the father, the law of the mother. Each proverb illustrated in the Bible or corroborated by direct teaching elsewhere,.

1—9 Wisdom and folly contrasted.

> 1:7 "Knowledge and wisdom far from being one
> Have oft-times no connection. Knowledge dwells
> In heads replete with thoughts of other men,
> Wisdom in minds attentive to their own.

Knowledge is proud that he has learned so much.
Wisdom is humble that he knows no more."—Cowper

1:23-31 "These are the verses used by the Spirit of God to awaken me as a lad of 14, and I found peace in John 3:18."—H. A. Ironside

2:1-5 *receive, hide, incline, apply, criest, lift est up, seekest, searchest*—the only way to get the mind of God. See Ezra 7:10.

3 Personal piety and consistent living. Mercy and truth: consideration for others and integrity of heart before God and man.

4 Wisdom as a guide for human life.

4:12 "As thou goest step by step, I will open up the way before thee." Heb. trans.

4:23 Circulation of the blood implied.

5 Wisdom preserving from uncleanness.

8:12 Wisdom personified. "Christ the Wisdom of God." "God hath made Him to be unto us—Wisdom." 8:23 set up—anointed.

(1) Christ, the Anointed from eternity.
(2) When born into the world.
(3) At His baptism.
(4) In His Resurrection.

9:1-12 Wisdom's invitation.

9:13-18 Folly's invitation.

10—24 Proverbs set in order by Solomon. The walk through this world of the one who is a disciple of Wisdom.

10:27-32 Righteousness and lawlessness contrasted.

11 Righteousness and lawlessness contrasted.

11:4 See the rich fool.

11:6 *righteousness*—hypocrite. See Job 8:13.

11:8 See Haman and Mordecai, Daniel and his accusers.

11:24 "A man there was, though some did count him mad;

> The more he cast away the more he had.
> It never was loving that emptied a heart
> Nor giving that emptied a purse." See ch. 13:7.

12—13 The love of knowledge in contrast to hatred of reproof.

12:9 *he that honoureth himself*—How many are of this type!

12:20 Note why people imagine evil concerning others.

14 The wise and the simple contrasted. 14:1 See the prudent woman of chapter 31.

14:14 Only place "backslider" is found in Bible.

14:32 The hope of immortality.

15 The tongue.

15:2 Wisdom, the ability to use knowledge aright.

16 The divine sovereignty—"Man proposes, God disposes."

16:15 The latter rain, a special blessing. See Jer. 3:3.

17 Divine principles.

17:1 Amen! *sacrifices*—i.e., peace offerings.

17:17 A friend—ch. 18:24; ch. 27:10.

18 Warnings against folly in speech.

18:1 The self-seeking schismatic. Separation after a carnal order. Jude 16-17. *intermeddleth with all wisdom*— or, rageth against all sound wisdom.

18:10, 11 Contrast these two verses.

18:22 A wife, not merely a woman.

19 The path of truth and the way of self-will.

19:7 Job and his friends.

19:17 Loans that pay big interest!

20 Warnings against evil habits, vice, etc.

20:6-12 The test of purity.

20:17 There is nothing covered that shall not be manifested—then the bitterness!

20:24 See Jer. 10:23, 24.

20:25 *and after vows to make enquiry*—i.e., he does as his appetite dictates—then inquires of God afterwards.

20:27 Personality of the spirit in man. Ps. 78:8; Rom. 1:9.

21 The moral government of God.

21:13 1 John 3:17. Active benevolence a condition of answered prayer.

21:18 On the Cross it was just the opposite.

21:31 The horse as a type. See Job 39:19; Rev. 6. 22—24:22 Exhortations to integrity and subjection to God.

22:6 *Train up*—dedicate, or initiate—Same word as in Deut. 20:5 (twice); 1 Kings 8:63; 2 Chron. 7:5.

22:17-18 Importance of studying the Word of God—2 Tim. 2:15; 2 Tim. 3:16; Luke 1:1-4.

24:11-12 Responsibility for men who know not God. Contrast Isa. 58:10.

24:23-34 An appendix to the division.

24:30-34 The field of the slothful. A fitting epilogue to this division.

25—29 Division 3—Later proverbs arranged by the men of Hezekiah. See 1 Kings 4:32.

25:7 Used by our Lord in Luke 14:8, 10.

25:21-22 Quoted in Romans 12:20.

25:25 The gospel likened to water. Rev. 22:17.

26 Fools and sluggards.

27:1 See Pharaoh in Ex. 8:10. Tomorrow—reasons for not delaying:
(1) Death may ensue.
(2) The Spirit may cease to strive.
(3) The Lord may return.
(4) We add to what we can never undo.
(5) We lose time we can never make up.

27:16 Impossible to shield her for she invariably betrays herself.

27:23 A word to pastors.

28:9 When it is no use to pray. See Isa. 1:15.

30 Division 4—The words of Agur.

30:24-28 Four Wise Things.

31 Division 5—The words of Lemuel.

Old Testament -- Ecclesiastes – Daniel

Ecclesiastes

Man's wisdom shown to be foolishness. The world by wisdom knew not God. *Under the sun*—29 times. *Vanity*—37 times. *Under the heavens*—3 times. *Upon the earth*—7 times. God's inspired record of what Solomon said in his heart as he considered things under the sun. Do the pleasures of life really compensate for the energy spent in obtaining them?

1:1-11 Prologue.

1:3 The? of the Book.

1:7 See 2 Cor. 9:8-11.

1:9 *no new thing under the sun*—the awful "sameness" of natural law.

1:12-15 Introduction. Fully qualified to make the test and see if there is happiness under the sun. 1 Kings 4:29.

1:16—4:16 The search for lasting good.

1:16-18 Wisdom does not satisfy.

2:3 Pleasure does not satisfy.

2:4 Architecture.

2:5 Agriculture.

2:6 Irrigation systems.

2:7 The comforts that wealth can give. Power and authority.

2:8 [first part] "Money is a universal provider for everything but happiness." [last part] The liberal arts.

2:12 Pleasures of learning philosophy. Materialism—living for the present.

3:1-8 Fatalism. The eternal circle of life.

Nothing abides—all moves—life is like a great wheel ever revolving.

3:14 The works of God distinguished from the puny efforts of man.

3:16 Legalized wickedness.

3:18 The conclusion of the natural man when he only looks "under the sun."

3:21 See the answer in ch. 12:7.

4:1 Injustice and oppression.

4:10 The Second Man lifts up the first man!

5—11 Considerations and conclusions based on experience.

5:1 Reverence.

5:4-5 Vows—See Num. 30. Integrity.

5:13-20 Philosophical conclusions but the heart still unsatisfied. See Job 1:21.

5:18-20 Moderation.

6:6 [last clause] i.e., the grave.

7—11 Commendation of morality.

7:1-8 Note the seven comparisons.

7:26 The love of women cannot satisfy.

7:28 And he had 1000 wives and concubines!

8 Commendation of wisdom.

8:8 But Christ, when His work was done, "dismissed His Spirit."

8:10 See the case of Joram—2 Chron. 21:20.

9 The philosophy of self-expression.

9:1 [last part] The Douay translates "no man knoweth whether he is worthy of favor or hatred."

9:5 Not Annihilation—but a fact so far as one can see "under the sun." know not anything—See I Sam. 20:39; 2 Sam. 15:11. Text used by materialists. Link with Job 3:13, 16; 10:18; 20:6-8; Ps. 39:13; 6:5; Isa. 38:18; Ps. 146:3, 4; 49:19, 20; Mal. 4:1-3. Note that these texts only have to do with man and the things of earth—the death is that of the body—and so far as man under the sun can see he disappears forever. But Christ brought life and incorruptibility to light through the gospel.

9:14-15 The forgotten deliverer. A glimpse of Christ!

10 Commendation of sobriety, integrity, moderation, etc.

10:4 Yieldingness. Phil. 4:5.

10:8 There is a law of retribution in life that man cannot turn aside.

10:15 Unable to find the way.

10:16 See Isa. 3:4 and 12.

11:1 See v. 6. See Isa. 32:20.

11:2 The highest conclusions of human wisdom.

12 God should be sought for Himself alone.

12:3 *keepers*—hands *strong*—legs *grinders*—teeth *look out of*—eyes	All Failing

12:4 *doors shall be shut*—ears *grinding*—eating **12:5** *almond tree*—white hair **12:6** *silver cord*—spinal cord *golden bowl*—brain *pitcher*—heart [last part] circulation of the blood	

12:7 The Spirit whether of the saved or lost has to do directly with God—the Father of Spirits—the God of the spirits of all flesh.

12:14 The Day of Judgment. Rom. 1:32.

Song Of Solomon

The Book of Communion—the mutual love of the king and his bride—Solomon a type of Christ. Eph. 5:25-26.

A maiden of Israel—a shepherdess whose heart is won by a stranger-shepherd who is really the king of Israel.

1:1—3:5 Division 1—The rapture of first love. 1 The bride of the king—The soul's awakening.

1:6 *black*—i.e., sunburnt.

1:7 Question 1—Seven questions asked in this song. See ch. 3:3.

1:13-17 With the king in the bower—conjugal love.

2 The soul's appreciation.

2:8-10 The shepherd's fiancee waiting for the coming of the bridegroom.

3 The soul's yearning.

3:1-4 She dreams that she is searching for her shepherd-lover.

3:3 [last part] Question 2—See ch. 3:6.

3:4 *I held him*—As the babe clings to its mother—but it is the mother's arms that hold it.

3:6—5:1 Division 2—Nuptial rejoicing.

3:6 The king comes to claim her. Question 3—See ch. 5:3. Heaven today is filled with the fragrance of the Cross of Christ. It is the Lord in resurrection here in view.

4 The soul's approval.

4:1-7 The shepherd-king expresses his delight in his bride.

4:8 Communion and separation. The "honeymoon."

Shenir—part of Mount Hermon. See Deut. 3:9; 1 Chron. 5:23; Ezek. 27:5.

4:12-15 The enclosed well-watered garden—Gen. 2:10; Isa. 58:11; Jer. 31:12.

4:16—5:16 The soul's fruitfulness and exercises.

5:2—8:14 Division 3—Separation and reunion.

5:2-8 She dreams again of communion interrupted.

5:3 Question 4—See ch. 5:9.

5:9 Question 5—See ch. 6:1 for part two.

6 The soul's delight. Communion restored.

6:1 Question 5, part two. See ch. 5:10.

6:10 Question 6. See ch. 8:5.

6:10-13 Reflecting him as she walks in his company.

6:13 Second part of question 6.

7 The soul's fellowship. Communion enjoyed.

7:5 Tresses—the glory of a woman is her hair.

7:11 Fellowship in loving service.

8 The soul's union.

The bride's sense of her inferiority—His gracious response. 8:5 Question 7.

8:6 Everlasting love—Jer. 31:3. See Ex. 28:29; John 15:13.

8:7 most vehement flame—flame of Jah.

8:11 Remembering the past.

Isaiah

1:12 Ch. 29:8.

1:13 Empty worship. Empty religion. Hos. 10:1; James 1:26; Matt. 15:9.

1:15 When it is no use to pray. Prov. 28:9.

2:2 Micah 4:1-3.

2:3 *Out of Zion.* See Rom. 11:26 and Isa. 27:9.

2:4 Contrast Joel 3:10.

2:19 See the sixth seal, Rev. 6.

5:8, 11, 18, 20, 21, 22;

6:5 Seven woes.

7:14 The Virgin's Son to be the sign of Judah's deliverance. But not in Ahaz' day. See ch. 9:6-7.

virgin—Almah found six other places in O.T. Gen. 24:43; Ex. 2:8; Ps. 68:25; Cant. 1:3; Cant. 6:8; Prov. 30:19. Always a pure maiden.

8:7 An army likened to a river. See ch. 18:2.

8:9 The last great confederation to be of no avail.

8:13-14 The stone identified with Jehovah.

8:19-20 Spiritism forbidden of God.

9:2 When the Light of World was there!

9:6 God manifest. Faith's appropriation of the promise of ch. 7:14.

10:5 The last Assyrian coming against Jerusalem in the days of the final apostasy under antichrist.

10:12 The Assyrian to be dealt with by God in the time of the end.

10:20 The restoration of the remnant of Israel in the last days.

10:24 The message to the remnant.

11:1 Messiah, the Branch. See Jer. 23:5.

11:2 The seven spirits of God. Rev. 1.

12:3 "Wells of Salvation." John 4 and John 7.

13:13 "Yet once more." See Heb. 12:26, 27.

13:19 Babylon's doom through the Medes—final—never to be restored.

14:2 [last part] Leading captivity captive—Ps. 68:18; Eph. 4:8, Judg. 5:12.

14:9-11 Consciousness in Sheol.

14:12 Lucifer's fall. See Ezek. 28:12.

14:25 The last Assyrian, the king of the north. Dan. 11.

15:5 [first part] Moab began at Zoar.

17:6 The vine and the olive tree never to be totally destroyed. See Rom. 11.

17:10 Palestine to be denuded of its forests and orchards.

18:2 *vessels* of *bulrushes*—vessels that suck up water.

19:3 [last part] Is this the Turk?

19:7 *paper reeds*—papyrus.

19:19 An altar in Egypt to Jehovah.

21:2 The advance of the Persians and Medes upon Babylon foreseen.

22:13 [last part] Also written by a Greek poet in later years.

22:14 [last part] Sin unto death.

22:22 See the letter to Philadelphia. Rev. 3.

23:15 *one king*—i.e., Nebuchadnezzar.

24:13 The remnant in the great tribulation.

25 A psalm of praise.

25:8 See Rev. 7.

26:12 "God that worketh in you." Phil. 2.

27:1 The binding of Satan. Rev. 20:1, 2.

27:3 Israel: Jehovah's vineyard again under His care.

27:13 The great trumpet. The true feast of trumpets at last!

28:10 Line upon line. See this illustrated in the frequent repetitions of the sacrificial ritual.

28:13 All God's instruction misused.

28:15 The 7-year covenant of Dan. 9. Ch. 24:5. See v. 18 of this chapter.

28:20 The restless sleeper.

29:8 The disappointed dreamer—empty lives and empty religion—Hos. 10:1; Isa. 1:13; Jas. 1:26.

29:10-12 The attitude of many towards the Book of Revelation—But see Rev. 22:10.

29:20-21 The reprover hated. Amos 5:10.

30:18 God *waits* till the right time. We must wait too.

30:21 Hos. 11:3 Guidance. Prov. 3:6. By the Word of God.

32:6 [last part], 8 Error cannot feed the soul, however much the intellect may delight in it.

32:17 Righteousness the ground of peace. Heb. 7:2.

32:20 Eccl. 11:1, 6.

34:4 Compare the sixth seal in Rev. 6.

34:5 See Zech. 13:7.

36—39 Historical parenthesis.

37:14 The letter of blasphemy. Contrast ch. 39:1.

38:20 The Jews call psalms 120 to 137 "Hezekiah's Song Book."

39 Letters and a present. Contrast 37:4.

40—48 Jehovah's controversy with idols.

40:8 1 Pet. 1:25.

40:9, 10, 13 The Trinity—v. 9 *your God.*—v. 10 *the Lord God* Jehovah, who is the Shepherd-King.—v. 13 *the Spirit of the Lord.* See ch. 48:16.

40:31 Eagles do not go in flocks. If you would mount up as an eagle, you must be willing to go alone.

41:21, 22 Jehovah's challenge to the idol priests and the false prophet.

41:23 "Things to come" only to be made known by the Spirit of God.

43:9-12 Israel's history, the witness to the truth of the prophetic word. See also ch. 44:8.

43:13 2 Thess. 2:6. 44:3 Water and the Spirit.

45:2 Christ can make all our crooked places straight.

45:3 He opens the doors by His omnipotent power. See the message to Philadelphia, Rev. 3.

45:13 Referring to Cyrus the Great.

45:15 See this illustrated in the Book of Esther.

45:18 The earth not created a waste—*bohu*—void—in vain— See Gen. 1:1, 2.

45:22 Look—Heb. panah—to turn. To look to Him is to trust—to turn from all else.

46:1, 2 Fleeing from their foes with their idols. The gods of the heathen have to be carried. The true God carries His people.

46:9, 10 See Ps. 119:160.

46:13 Righteousness to be brought by the gospel.

47 Literal Babylon—compare spiritual Babylon in Rev. 17—18.

48:1 Pride of position, but in a wretchedly unspiritual condition.

48:5 Through Moses in Lev. 27.

48:12 See the Alpha and Omega in Rev. 1.

48:16 The divine Trinity.

48:17 See ch. 40:9-13.

48:18 Ps. 81.

48:22 The end of Jehovah's controversy with idols.

49—57 The rejection of the true servant of Jehovah.

49:3, 4 Christ taking His place as the true Israel.

49:5 Rejected by the nation.

49:6 A Saviour of the Gentiles.

49:12 Sinim is generally identified with China or the Far East.

49:14-17 Zion is ever before God and dear to His heart, even during all the years of Israel's blindness and the desolation of the land.

49:18-19 Future restoration and blessing.

49:22 The return to God and to the land in the last days.

50:4 Ps. 40:6. The ear opened.—Discipleship. See Ex. 21.

51:5 God's righteousness (Romans). See Isa. 46:12-13; 56:1.

52 The restoration of Israel to God and to the land in the new age.

52:3 See their complaint in Ps. 44:12.

52:13-15 The suffering Servant—His humiliation and exaltation.

53:1-3 The Servant before God and man.

53:4-6 The atoning Saviour.

53:7-9 His mock trial, death, and burial.

53:9 His grave was appointed with the wicked but He lay with the rich in His death.

53:10-12 The sinner's Substitute—His Resurrection and its results.

54 Israel's future blessing based on the atonement of Christ.

54:1 He suffered that His redeemed might be able to sing for joy.

55:1 The gospel invitation.

56:1 The righteousness of God. See ch. 46:13; 51:5; 59:16.

56:8 *other sheep have I.*—John 10.

56:10 *dumb dogs—Beware of dogs*—Phil. 3:2.

57:15 *Eternity*—Only place in the English Bible.

57:19 *the fruit of the lips*—Heb. 13:15; Ps. 119:108.

58—66 The end of the Lord's controversies with Israel— Their restoration, conversion, and millennial blessing.

58:9 Conditions upon which God answers prayer. Contrast Prov. 24:11-12.

58:11 *a watered garden*—Gen. 2:10; Isa. 27:2-3; Cant. 4:15; Jer. 31:12.

59:5, 6 *adder's eggs and spider's webs*—Ps. 58:4; Ps. 140:3. See Job 8:14.

59:19 The restrainer. 2 Thess. 2.

60 Millennial glory following upon the repentance of Israel.

61:1-3 The anointed Saviour: 1—the anointing, 2—the purpose of the anointing, 3—the results of the preaching.

61:3 ashes—All the joys of life have burnt out.

62:1 The burning lamp. See Gen. 15:17.

62:5 [last part] Canticles.

63 Judgment on the nations that have rejected the gospel —the precursor to Israel's blessing.

63:10-14 The Holy Spirit in the O.T. A divine person who might be "vexed" and who led the people and was "put within" some of them. See note at Eph. 4:32. The Spirit of God in the wilderness (Neh. 9:20); in Moses —and with the people in the land.

64 Confession and prayer of the remnant.

64:1 Removing mountains—Matt. 21:21, 23; Mark 11:23; Zech. 4:7.

65:3 *altars of brick*—human limitations.

66:4 [first clause] judicial darkness. 2 Thess. 2.

66:5 High exclusive claims.

66:7 Israel the mother of the man-child. Rev. 12; Jer. 4:31.

66:17 Sanctified to do iniquity.

Jeremiah

Jeremiah prophesied prior to the finding the book of the Law (2 Chron. 34) in the days of Josiah—and continued to the end of Judah's occupation of the land—100 years later than Isaiah. Later than Hosea, Joel, Amos, Micah, Nahum, Jonah. Contemporary with Zephaniah, Habakkuk, Obadiah, and Ezekiel. Daniel studied Jeremiah (Dan. 9).

1—24 Division 1—Jehovah's pleading with His erring people—"A vessel chosen and fitted."

1:5 Jeremiah's call.

1:6 Compare with Moses.

1:9 Isaiah's was the touch of cleansing. Jeremiah's is the touch of power.

1:10 Note the authority connected with the prophetic office. Consider Paul—Peter—Savonarola—Gregory of Armenia—John Knox—Calvin—Luther—etc.

1:11 *almond tree*—"hastening tree."

1:12 The pledge of reassurance.

1:13-16 The judgment Judah must endure from the north— Chaldea, etc. 2—3:5 Entreaty and warning.

2:2 Their first love. Connect with "Ephesus" in Rev. 2.

2:7 Contrast with our inheritance—1 Pet. 1:4.

2:13 See John 4:14; 7:37, 39—God Himself will break every cistern we make if we forsake Him.

2:17 Reaping as they sowed.

2:24 The wild ass—the unregenerate man.

2:26 Not ashamed of the sin, but of its discovery.

2:27-28 No right to count on God in the day of trouble if not walking with Him before the trouble comes.

3:3 Deut. 11:14—The latter rain withheld because of idolatry. See ch. 5:24.

3:6—6:30 Future glory conditioned upon repentance.

3:7 Only one king of Israel is said to have sought the Lord— Jehoahaz. 2 Kings 13:4, 5.

3:8-11 There was much that was unreal in the great revival under Josiah.

3:12-13 Confession demanded as a prelude to blessing.

3:16 Last mention of the Ark in the O.T.

3:19 [first part] Repentance predicted—The Need of New Birth.

4:1-2 The need of reality. Jehovah's response to the cry of anguish in the previous chapter.

4:3 A good word for the evangelist!

4:5-13 Vision of the invading army. Nebuchadnezzar and his Chaldean army. 4:14 The only door of escape unheeded, so the judgment must fall.

4:23-31 The coming desolation of the land at the Babylonian conquest and at the time of the end.

5:1 Looking for one to stand in the breach.

5:14 See the two witnesses of Rev. 11:5. Jer. 20:9.

5:18-21 Judah to be carried back to the very land from which God had called Abraham, because of unfaithfulness to the truth.

5:24 Ch. 3:3—Israel exhorted to recognize the Giver of the latter rain—See Hos. 6:3.

5:30-31 The apostate condition fully exposed.

6:1 Call to separation addressed to the Benjamites.

6:4 The declining day!

6:14 No peace.

6:15 No shame.

6:16 The *old* way and the *old* paths—See Prov. 14:12.

6:18 The nation called to witness the righteousness of the Lord's dealings.

7—10 "What agreement hath the Temple of God with idols?" Judgment must begin at the house of God.

7:1-7 The defilement of the sanctuary.

7:4 No time for high exclusive claims.

7:5-7 Great pretensions while neglecting righteousness—2 Tim. 2:22—"Follow righteousness."

7:8-16 The divorce of position from condition.

7:11 Referred to by our Lord in Matt. 21:13, linked with Isa. 56:7.

7:12 Jerusalem to be left desolate as Shiloh.

7:16 *Sin unto death*—Too late for prayer to be of any avail.

7:17-20 The Babylonian cult set up in Jerusalem. Astarte or Ashtaroth (Semiramis) worship.

7:21-28 Sacrifices of no value while living in sin.

7:28 No heed to the prophetic message.

7:29-34 Terrible retribution coming.

7:31 The origin of Gehenna (outside Jerusalem) used by Christ as a picture of eternal judgment. See ch. 19:4-8.

8:1-3 Unsparing judgment.

8:3 Choosing death. Deut. 30:19.

8:4-12 Jerusalem given up to perpetual backsliding.

8:6-19 Not saved v. 20 Why?
(1) Unrepentant v. 6.
(2) Unobservant v. 7—Nature would have instructed —but they heeded not.
(3) Pride of intellect—the Word rejected v. 8.
(4) Self-deceived v. n.
(5) Utterly shameless v. 12.
(6) Carnal optimism v. 15.
(7) Religious formality v. 19.

8:9 A word for modernists.

8:13-17 Unsparing judgment.

8:18-22 A lamentation over the awful state of the people.

8:20 *Not saved.*

8:22 Three Questions: Balm in Gilead.
1—Is there no remedy? Answer: God's Word: "He sent His Word and healed them"—Ps. 107:20. His wounds—"by His stripes—healed"—Isa. 53:5. His wings—"healing in His wings"—Mai. 4:2. His ways—"as they went—healed"—Luke 17:14.
2—Is there no physician? Answer: Christ.
3—Why not healed? The remedy refused.

9:1-8 Jeremiah's identification with the erring people.

9:9-11 Jerusalem's desolation.

9:12-16 A challenge to consider these things.

9:17-22 Time to mourn.

9:23-24 True glory is to know the Lord.

9:25-26 "No difference."

10 The Folly of Idolatry—Compare Isa. 44.

10:23 Self-judgment—Prov. 4:26; 5:21; 20:24.

11—12 The burned branches and the swelling of Jordan. Jehovah's expostulation—ch. 11.

11:4 The iron furnace—See Abraham's vision—Gen. 15:17. [last part] Law—demands then gives. Grace gives and beseeches.

11:11 Useless to pray if determined upon disobedience—Jer. 14:11.

11:14 Sin unto death—1 John 5:16.

11:16 The olive tree—compare with Rom. 11:16-26.

11:18-20 Jeremiah speaks for the godly remnant. The tree to be preserved though the branches be destroyed.

12 Jeremiah's intercession—Compare with Hab. 1:12.

13 The marred girdle—the girdle the sign of service— Israel set aside as an unprofitable servant and must be carried to Babylon.

13:9-10 Judah to be carried to the valley of the Euphrates and chastised there for the sin of idolatry.

13:16
Natural *darkness*—Ephesians.
Wilful *darkness*—John 3.
Judicial *darkness*—Jeremiah 15.
Eternal *darkness*—Jude.

Judicial darkness because of light rejected. Compare with 2 Thess. 2:11, 12—Isa. 66:4.

13:18 Jehoiakim and his consort directly addressed.

13:23 The trouble is in the nature of man.

14 Dialogue between God and Jeremiah.

14—15 Famine—temporal and spiritual.

14:1-6 The real famine was within.

14:7-9 Confession and prayer.

14:10-12 God's answer.

14:11 Too late for prayer.

14:13-17 False prophets give false comfort.

14:17-2 2 The prophet's complaint.

15:1-9 Jehovah's answer.

15:1 No hope of deliverance.

15:4 Literally fulfilled.

15:10 Jeremiah's complaint.

Separation the path of the faithful.

15:11-14 Jehovah's answer.

15:15-18 Jeremiah's protestation.

15:16 The Word and the Name—Eating the Word—See Ezek. 3:1-3—Rev. 10:8-11.

15:19-21 Jehovah's promise.

15:20 The separated man a witness for God.

15:21 Redemption.

16—17 Apostasy till there is no remedy.

16:7 The O.T. reference to the breaking of bread. See Ps. 45:17.

16:14-15 The predicted return—See ch. 31:36.

17:1 Sin where the blood should be—See Lev. 4:7, 18, 2 5 and 30.

17:9 The deceitful heart of man—Illustration: Benedict Arnold wrote Miss Shippen, afterwards his 2d wife: "I daily discover so much baseness and ingratitude among mankind, that I almost blush at being of the same species."

7:20-27 The sabbath a test of the true condition of the people.

18—19 Lessons from the potter's house.

18:1-17 The message.

18:14 [last clause] i.e., Had the snows of Lebanon ceased to supply the cold flowing spring?

18:18-23 The message rejected.

19 The second message.

19:6 Tophet: the Valley of Hinnom. Gehenna—See ch. 7:31.

20 Pashur the false prophet opposes.

20:2 Jeremiah arrested.

20:14 Compare with Job 3.

21—24 The siege and captivity foretold.

21:2 When it is no use to pray—See Prov. 1.

22 The doom of the kings of Judah. Four false shepherds to be destroyed.

22:11 *Shallum*—referring to Shallum or Jehoahaz, who had been carried to Egypt.

22:30 [first part] The curse of Coniah: If Jesus were Joseph's natural son He would be barred from the throne of David, but as Son of Mary by divine generation He inherits the throne. See the two genealogies— Matt, 1 and Luke 3.

23 The true King.

23:18 Quoted from in 1 Cor. 2:16.

23:21 False prophets misleading a credulous people.

23:28-29 The Word of God in contrast to idle dreams. Fire and hammer.

24 The good and bad figs. A judicial summing up.

25—51 Division 2—Judgment executed because the people refuse to hearken.

25 The seventy years' captivity foretold.

25:11 The seventy years' servitude. See Dan. 9:2. Distinguish between the 70 years' servitude and the 70 years' desolations.

25:29 Compare 1 Pet. 4:17.

26 Danger and deliverance.

26:11 Indignation against the "pessimist."

27—28 Bonds and yokes.

27:1 *Jehoiakim*—See R. V. Zedekiah—copyist's error.

27:6 The beginning of the times of the Gentiles. See Dan. 2. The head of gold. For the end, see Luke 21.

27:15 Linking the sacred Name with their own dreamings —See ch. 29:9.

27:22 The return of the vessels. See Ezra 1.

28 The false prophet, Hananiah.

28:3, 11 Time prophecies always a trap unless the prophet be divinely inspired.

29 The prophet's letter to the first of the captivity (under Jehoiachin). The seventy years are the length of one Babylonian empire. They began B.C. 606 with the servitude of 2 Kings 24:1.

29:14 The predicted return, ch. 30:3.

30—31 Dispensational—Jacob's trouble and the restoration to follow.

30:7 The great tribulation—Matt. 24; Rev. 7.

31:15 Fulfilled when Herod sought to kill the infant Jesus.

31:20 See the entire prophecy of Hosea.

31:31 The new covenant—Heb. 10. Note—It is to be made with Israel and Judah—not with the Church.

31:36 Israel's Restoration. See Ezek. 36:23. The unbreakable covenant. See ch. 23:35.

31:38-40 The new city—See Zech. 14:10. The corner of Hananeel has already been uncovered.

32—33 Jeremiah's imprisonment.

32:10 The sealed title deed.

32:11 Key to the sealed book in Rev. 5.

32:17 Answer to God's question—Gen. 18:14.

32:35 They would do for their idols what they would never do for God and what He would never ask of them.

34 Bondage in place of liberty. A jubilee proclaimed and then rescinded.

35 The house of the Rechabites.

36 The Word of God rejected.

36:23 The man who knifed the Word of God! The first destructive critic on record.

36:32 Compare and contrast—Rev. 22:18, 19.

37—39 The fall of Jerusalem.

37:3, 17 No use to pray when walking in disobedience.

38:4 What passes for patriotism in opposition to God's truth.

38:7 The faithfulness of Ebed-melech: a Negro.

38:19 "The fear of man bringeth a snare."

39:7 The man who *would not* see when he could, now cannot see when he would. Ezek. 12:13.

40—44 The remnant left in the land. 40:14 Gedaliah—a guileless man.

41 Ishmael's treachery.

41:6 What a hypocrite!

41:17 *Chimham*—Tradition connects this with the inn in which Jesus was born.

42:2-3 Insincere in their request. No use to pray if there be not reality. See v. 20.

43:4 Wilful disobedience in going down to Egypt.

44:3-4 Idolatry—the sin that God hated above all others.

44:15-19 The folly of depending on experience in place of obedience to the Word of God. A common mistake in all dispensations. Faith in, and obedience to the Word of God. See ch. 7:18-19.

45 The Word to Baruch.

46—49 God's Word to the nations.

46:2 Egypt (1).

46:7-8 Armies symbolized by rivers and overflowing floods.

46:27-28 Israel to be punished but preserved by God.

47:1 Philistia (2).

47:6 The sword of the Lord—Zech. 13:7—Ezek. 21:3.

48:1 Moab (3).

48:37 Hair—the strength of nature.

48:38 *vessel wherein is no pleasure*—Rom. 9. Vessels of wrath.

48:45 See the prophecy of Balaam—Num. 21:28.

48:46-47 Moab's doom—compare the prophecy of Balaam—Num. 24:17.

49:1 Ammon (4).

49:2 [last part] Captivity to be led captive.

49:7 Edom (5). Connect with Obadiah.

49:11 Insurance—A wonderful promise in the midst of words of judgment.

49:23 Syria (6).

49:28 Arabia (7).

49:34 Elam (8).

50—51 Doom of Babylon and Judah's deliverance.

50:15 Righteous retribution.

50:38 Babylon the mother of idolatry.

50:39 Literally fulfilled for many centuries.

51:6 The call to flee is given in mercy. It is not legal. See v. 45. Connect with Rev. 17.

51:20 Israel: Jehovah's battle ax.

51:25 Connect with Rev. 8:8.

51:37-39 All literally fulfilled through the centuries.

51:45 The call to separation. See v. 6.

52 Historical appendix by another hand. Compare with ch. 39.

52:28 The servitude.

52:29 The captivity.

52:30 The desolations.

Lamentations

The prophet's grief over the fulfilment of what he had himself predicted. The Spirit of Christ entering into all the afflictions of His people.

1 The desolations of Jerusalem. An acrostic—each verse starts with a letter of the Hebrew alphabet.

1:3 No rest!

1:6 No pasture!

1:9 No comforter!

1:12-13 The Spirit of Christ speaking in the prophet.

2 The day of the Lord's anger—Same acrostic form as ch. 1 and ch. 4.

2:4-5 As an adversary and an enemy—but not really one.

2:9 No Vision!

3 "Let us search and try our ways."

Full manifestation of Judah's fallen condition.

The prophet fully identifies himself with the people. Their sins are his, their woes are his. Their judgments are shared by him. A triple acrostic. Each section of 3 verses begins with the same letter in each verse.

3:8 See v. 44.

3:18-20 He will never forget the wormwood and the gall.

3:21 Hope in the midst of deep grief.

3:22-23 Subjection under discipline.

3:31-32 Confidence in God in the hour of trial.

3:40 Call to repentance.

4 The fine gold become dim. Acrostic as ch. 1 and 2.

4:19 "The lion with eagle's wings."

4:21 Connect with the prophecy of Obadiah.

5 Thou, O Lord remainest forever! The acrostic form is not followed in this chapter.

Ezekiel

The Sanctuary Book of the series—Ezekiel the priest leading us into the presence of God. Division 1—Prophecies prior to the destruction of Jerusalem—Chapters 1 to 32. Division 2—Prophecies after the destruction of Jerusalem—Chapters 33 to 48.

1—24 Section 1—Judgments concerning Jerusalem.

1—3:14 The vision of the glory of God and the call to the prophetic office.
The vision of the divine government. God is over all and in all. The human linked with and controlled by the divine. Winged directness. There are no second causes to the eye of the man of faith.

1:3 *the hand of the Lord was there upon him*—This phrase found seven times: ch. 1:3; 3:14, 22; 8:1; 33:22; 37:1; 40:1.

1:4 The divine chariot.

1:5 The cherubim. Intelligence—the universe is not at the mercy of chance.

1:7 *brass*—judgment.
feet—winged stability, a sure foot.

1:10 face of a man—Luke.
face of a lion—Matthew.
face of an ox—Mark—ox literally cherub. See ch. 10:4.
face of an eagle—John.
the man—intelligence.
the lion—strength and majesty.
the ox—stability, dependableness, service.
the eagle—Providence, swiftness in judgment, perception.
"Reason, courage, patience, aspiration, all are winged: touched with the divine."

1:15-21 The wheels of the divine chariot. God's ways with men on the earth.

1:16 Wheels within wheels—His ways past finding out.

1:19 No turning aside the divine government.

1:26 A Man upon the throne. "We see Jesus, crowned with glory and honor."

1:28 Compare with Isa. 6:1-10.

2:1 Collapse—the result of coming into the presence of God.

2:3-8 The call to the prophetic office. Ezekiel's commission. Compare with Isaiah, Moses, Jeremiah, Daniel, Peter, etc.

2:8 Eating the Book. Compare with John in Rev. 10 and with Jer. in ch. 15:16.

3:3 The Word must enter into the inward parts.

3:15—7:2 7 The judgment announced. Four signs.

3:17 Commissioned to be a watchman.

3:18-19 Compare with Paul to the Ephesian elders, Acts 20.

4:1-3 The first acted-out sermon.

4:4-8 The second acted-out sermon.

4:5 390 Days of Israel's apostasy.

4:6 40 Days—Judah's apostasy.

4:9-12 The third acted-out sermon.

4:12 *bake it with*—Note: Not mingle with but use as part of the fuel.

4:15 Cattle chips as fuel. 5:1-4 The fourth acted-out sermon.

5:5 Jerusalem always in the center of the stage, as God views the nations.

5:14-15 All the centuries since have witnessed the truth of this prophecy.

8—11 Visions relating to Jerusalem.

8:2 *fire*—"of a man." In Heb. esh is "fire" and ish is "man." See Rev. 10.

8:10 Creeping things and beasts of all kinds put in the place of God. Rom. 1.

8:11 Shaphan the scribe who received from Hilkiah the book of the law found in the Temple—2 Kings 22:8-11; Jer. 39:14.

8:12 "Character is what a man is in the dark."

8:14 Tammuz the son of Nimrod, called by the Babylonians Dumuzi—The god of spring vegetation who dies, goes to Hades, and returns in spring—Easter.

9 The man with the inkhorn—Sealing of the faithful ones—As in the coming great tribulation.

The Word for *mark* is *tav*—the last letter of the Hebrew alphabet. Formerly written as a cross.

9:6 1 Pet. 4:17.

10 The coals of fire.

10:2 Connect with Rev. 8:5.

10:4 The slow departure of the Shekinah from the Temple.

10:8 The angel of the covenant. 10:12 The eyes of the Lord searching out evil.

10:14 *cherub*—Note that what was before the face of an ox is now an angel!

10:18 The glory moving away in the divine chariot.

11 Judgment on the leaders.

11:13 Suddenly destroyed—no remedy.

11:16-19 God to be the sanctuary of the scattered nation. Their restoration promised when they shall be born again. John 3.

11:22-24 Ichabod—the Shekinah on the Mt. of Olives. Complete withdrawal. Whence the Lord Himself went up!

12—19 Signs, messages, and parables.

12:1-6 The sign of the evacuation of Jerusalem.

12:13 [last part] Zedekiah blinded by the king of Babylon. Jer. 39:7.

12:17-20 Sign of the affliction that was to come.

12:21-28 Judgment not to be delayed.

13 Against false prophets and prophetesses.

14:3 Useless to pray with idols in the heart. See ch. 20:2, 3.

14:21 See the 2d, 3d, and 4th seals of Rev. 6.

15 Parable of the unfruitful vine—Contrast with the True Vine in John 15.

16 Parable of the abandoned child.

16:3 i.e., Jerusalem originally a Canaanitish city, Jebus.

16:6-14 It is all what He did!

16:10 Only reference to badgers' skin apart from the Tabernacle. Really dolphin or seal skin, impervious to the elements. Typical of separation sanctification. The feet protected from defilement.

16:26 Egypt—type of the world, great of flesh. See Jas. 4:4.

16:55 No reference to eternal conditions but earthly blessing—which Judah had forfeited, as had Sodom and Samaria.

17 Parable of the two eagles, the cedar, and the vine.

17:3 *great eagle* — Nebuchadnezzar.

highest branch of the cedar—Jehoiakim.

7:5 Zedekiah.

17:7 *another great eagle*—Pharaoh Hophra, king of Egypt.

17:9 The Egyptian alliance of no avail to ward off the judgment.

18 God's judgments are in righteousness.

Sour grapes. Putting the blame on God as in Ex. 34:7. Principles of the divine government. The Divine Government. Not Soul Salvation. See also ch. 33. Life for obedience. This is governmental law, not the gospel.

18:32 2 Pet. 3:9—God's desire for all men. See ch. 9 Lamentation over the princes of Israel.

20—24 Final predictions concerning the doom of Jerusalem.

20 Arraignment of the nation for its unfaithfulness. To be chastened for their sins but restored to the Lord in the last days.

20:3 No use to pray—See Jer. 21:1-7; Ezek. 14:3.

20:33 The future restoration.

20:35 The wilderness of the people.

20:47 The green and the dry trees. See ch. 17:24; Hos. 10:8.

21 The impending judgment—The sword song.

21:3 Zech. 13:7.

21:5 The sword that was sheathed in the heart of Jesus.

21:10 How can man make mirth with judgment like a sword hanging over him?

21:16 Decide!

21:21 Literally, "he shook his arrows" in the divination ceremony.

21:25 *thou profane wicked prince of Israel*—Zedekiah type of antichrist. Literally, "O deadly wounded one, the prince of Israel."

21:26 The crown reserved for the Man of God's counsels — Connect with Hos. 3.

22 Jerusalem's abominations.

22:7-13 Note how he rings the changes on in thee.

22:12 Matt. 23:37.

22:14 Two solemn questions. See Job 9:4.

22:30 No mediator.

23:25 [first part] *Nose* and *ears* taken away. Impossible now to discern or hear the mind of God.

24 The final message.

24:2 The very date of the beginning of the siege made known by the Spirit.

24:25-27 The prophet to be dumb till tidings came of Jerusalem's fall—See ch. 33:22.

25—32 Judgments upon the nations.

25:2 Ammon (1).

25:8 Moab (2). Jer. 48:29.

25:12 Edom (3). God had commanded Israel to be kind to Edom—Deut. 23:7.

25:15 Philistia (4).

26:2 *Tyre* (5) *rock*. First mentioned in Josh. 19:29 as "the strong city."

26:4 Literally fulfilled.

27:5 Senir—i.e., Hermon. See Deut. 3:9; 1 Chron. 5:23; Cant. 4:8.

27:14 *Togarmah*—Armenia.

28:2 Type of the antichrist—2 Thess. 2.

28:12-16 No human king. Satan's former estate and his fall—See John 8:44 and Isa. 14:12.

28:15 Satan an apostate.

28:16 Here the personal description ends.

28:17 Tyre again before the mind of the prophet. The city has followed the lead of the "king." "The condemnation of the devil."

28:20 Zidon (6).

29:1 Egypt (7).

29:3 Pharaoh—type of Satan. The river the source of Egypt's life, yet God is not acknowledged.

30:3 The time of the heathen. Connect with "the times of the Gentiles." Luke 21:24.

30:13 No prince of Egyptian blood to sit on Egypt's throne—yet there is a king of the south in the time of the end.

31:6 Compare with Daniel 4 and the parable of the mustard tree.

32 The funeral dirge over Pharaoh—Hophra.

32:17 An elegy over Egypt.

32:21 Hell is Sheol, the unseen world.

33—48 Part 2—Predictions after the destruction of Jerusalem.

33—44 Section 1—The watchman and the shepherds.

33:11 2 Pet. 3:9. God's desire that all men should be saved. See 1 Tim. 2:4; Matt. 23:37; Luke 13:34; Ezek. 18:32.

33:18-20 Summary of the principles of the divine government. God's governmental ways with men in the flesh. The principle laid down in Ex. 34 still holds good. The divine government. God is ever true to His Word—but none can establish his own righteousness so God makes another change and gives the individual who repents a promise of mercy and declares He will judge those who sin against Him. It is law still. Life (on this earth) for obedience is not the gospel, which is "believe and live."

33:21 Tidings of Jerusalem's fall confirming the prophetic word.

33:24 Their idle boast when they lacked the faith of Abraham.

33:30 Hearing but not acting on what they hear.

33:32 Entertained but not exercised.

34:2 The false shepherds to be judged. The Lord Himself, the Good Shepherd. Connect with John 10.

34:8 The false shepherds.

34:10 "As they that must give an account." 1 Peter 5:2-3.

34:11 The Good Shepherd.

34:20 Jehovah the Saviour.

34:23 The Coming Redeemer—The true Shepherd—Jer. 30:9; Hos. 3:5.

34:26 "Showers of blessing." The times of refreshing—Acts 3:19, 20.

35—36 Section 2—Judgments upon Mt. Seir—and Israel's restoration predicted.

36 Promises of grace for Israel following judgment on their enemies.

36:17 Contrast 1 Peter 1:4—"undeniable."

36:21 See Rom. 2:24.

36:23-38 Note the "I will's" (18).

37—48 Future blessing of Israel. Millennial conditions following the great tribulation.

37:1-3 A scene of death: man's state as God beholds it. Life in the message: "I am come that they might have life." Compare with Dan. 12:2.

37:5 Bones are no obstacle to the bonemaker.

37:9-10 The breath in the winds and the voice of God in all circumstances. Life is in the Word.

37:24 One Shepherd. Note that in John 10 the saved from the Gentiles "other sheep" are to be part of the flock of the same Good Shepherd.

38 The great northern confederation of the last days. Compare with the predictions of the Assyrian of the end times—Isa. 10; Micah 5:5. Note that these are largely nations outside of the Roman empire.

38:2 chief prince—Prince of Rosh, i.e., Russia.

38:15 Typical Cossack troops.

38:22 Either natural hailstones, etc., or perhaps bombing from airplanes.

39:9 Seven years burning the weapons of war.

39:12 Seven months burying the dead of the great invading army.

39:17 The doom of the northern invader. See "the great supper of God" in Rev. 19.

39:23-29 Millennial blessing for Israel. The last foe defeated.

40—48 The vision of the millennial temple and its worship.

40—42 Section 1—The sanctuary.

40:1 *beginning of the year*—Rosh Hoshanah.

fourteenth year—B.C. 572. 40:2 Compare with the vision of the heavenly Jerusalem from a "very high mountain" in Rev. 21.

41 The inner sanctuary.

41:18 Two faces—intelligence and majesty.

41:22 [last part] The altar called the table. See 1 Cor. 10.

41:26 *narrow*—closed.
thick planks—the portals.

42:6 *straitened*—narrowed, i.e., the stories were terraced.

43—46 Section 2—The temple worship in the coming age.

43:10 The vision intended to provoke to repentance that the soul may be ashamed.

43:12 Holiness the law of the house of God.

44:31 The priestly food: the One who voluntarily went into death. "No man taketh My life from Me." I lay it down of myself.

45:20 The "simple" one covered by the blood of atonement.

45:21-23 The passover in the millennium. The memorial of the work of the Cross.

46:13-15 Continual memorial of the death of Christ and the recognition of the perfection of His Person.

47—48 Section 3—The regeneration of the land of Israel.

47 The vision of the living waters—Joel 3:18; Zech. 14:8. This river runs all through the Scriptures. Gen. 2:10; Ps. 36:8; 46:4; 65:9; Isa. 58:11; Song of Sol. 4:15; Isa. 27:2, 3.

"Before the prophet could tell others of the river he had to be brought into it himself." Dolman.

"As long as you remain in the stream you have clean feet." Dolman. 1 Sam. 2:9.

"Cleansing of the daily walk." Always in the stream.

Compare with the *pure river of water of life, clear as crystal* in Rev. 22. Wherever God rests a river flows forth to bless mankind.

47:3 The walk in the Spirit—"up to the ankles."

47:4 *knees*—praying in the Spirit.

to the loins—working in the Spirit.

47:5 *to swim in*—all for God. Life in the fullness of the Spirit.

47:10 En-gedi, En-eglaim—at the two ends of the Dead Sea.

47:11-12 Chemicals to be obtained from the Dead Sea district. Compare the river of Rev. 22.

48:30-35 Answering to the gates in the heavenly city above. See Rev. 21.

Daniel

1:8 Purpose of heart. See Acts 11:23.

2:18-19 Prayer—ministry—worship.

2:21 God changes the "times and seasons." See Acts 1:7; 1 Thess. 5:1.

2:31 The image of "the times of the Gentiles."

2:35 [last part] Matt. 21:44.

2:36-45 The interpretation.

2:38 Babylon.

2:39 Medo-Persia—Greco-Macedonia.

2:40 Roman.

2:41 The nations in the last days.

2:42 *toes of the feet*—the ten kingdoms. Rev. 13 and 17.

2:45 "The stone that will fall from heaven."

3:12 *certain Jews*—the faithful remnant.

3:19 [last part] the great tribulation in figure.

3:27 Yielded bodies—Rom. 12:1.

5 Babylon's destruction typical of the overthrow of the false religious system in the time of the end. Rev. 17.

6:17 The sealed stone—as at the tomb of Christ.

7:1-15 The vision.

7:4 *lion*—Babylon.

7:5 *bear*—Medo-Persia.

7:6 *leopard*—Greece.

7:7 *fourth beast*—Rome.

7:8 The last monarch.

7:13 The kingdom of the Son of Man.

7:16-28 The interpretation.

7:19 The Roman empire.

7:20 The last ten kings.

7:21 The great tribulation.

7:24 The same as the ten toes on the image of chapter 2.

7:25 [last part] 3 ½ years.

8:5 Alexander the Great.

8:6 Darius Codomanus.

8:8 Alexander's empire broken into four parts. 8:9 Antiochus Epiphanes.

8:22 Cassander, king of Greece; Lysimachus, king of Thrace; Seleucus, king of Syria; Ptolemy, king of Egypt.

9 Prophetic years are 360 days each. 3 ½ years in the Apocalypse, 1260 days or 42 months of 30 days. So 483 years would be 173880—the exact number of days from Artaxerxes' decree to Palm Sunday.

9:2 Daniel a student of Jeremiah and Chronicles.

9:13 [last part] Understanding the truth is the result of turning from iniquity.

9:24 The backbone of prophecy.

9:27 The covenant between the beast and the antichrist.

See Isa. 28:15-18.

10:2 *three full weeks*—distinguished from the weeks of ch. 9:24— which were sevens of years.

10:5 [first part] The up-look changes all.

10:5-6 The majesty of God seen in His angel.

10:8 The breakdown of the prophet.

10:7-18 The collapse of man when he has a vision of God. Compare Abraham — Jacob — Moses — Joshua — Gideon — Manoah — Isaiah — Jeremiah — Job — Peter — John — Paul.

Note the 3 touches: 1—set on his knees, v. 10; 2— lips, v. 16; 3—touch of power, v. 18.

10:12 Conflict in the heavenlies—restraining the answer to prayer.

11 Porphyry declared this chapter must have been written after the events mentioned, so accurately are the wars and intrigues of the Ptolemies and the Seleucidse described. Prophecy is history prewritten. History is prophecy fulfilled. "All history is His story."

11:2 *three kings in Persia*—Cyrus, Cambyses, Darius Hystaspes. fourth—Xerxes.

11:3 *a mighty king*—Alexander the Great.

11:4 *four winds of heaven*—Cassander, Lysimachus, Seleucus, Ptolemy, after battle of Ipsus.

not to his posterity—Alexander left no heir. A posthumous son was murdered and the empire eventually divided among his four leading generals.

11:5 *king of the south*—Ptolemy Lagus succeeded by P. Soter. *have dominion*—Seleucus Nicator annexed Babylon and Media, etc.

11:6 Antiochus Theos married Berenice, daughter of P. Philadelphus, divorcing Laodice to do so.

11:7-8 *out of a branch of her roots*—Berenice murdered, her son Callinicus reigned. P. Euergetes came against him. He won a great victory. Outlived Callinicus by four years.

11:10 *his* [Callinicus'] sons—Ceraunus and Antiochus the Great attacked Egypt. Ceraunus died. Antiochus defeated by P. Philopater at battle of Raphia.

11:13 Antiochus the Great allied with Philip III of Macedon.

11:14 *the robbers of thy people*—Jewish apostates in army of Antiochus.

11:15-16 Antiochus defeated the Egyptian general Sco-pias at Paneas. Antiochus went to Egypt—won great victory, returned to Palestine.

1:16 *consumed*—perfected

11:17 [last part] Cleopatra daughter of Antiochus wedded to P. Epiphanes.

11:18-19 Isles of Aegean Sea subdued by Antiochus. Greeks sought aid of Romans. Lucius Scipio defeated A.—Antiochus slain while attempting to rob a temple of Jupiter at Elymais.

11:20 *a raiser of taxes*—Seleucus Philopater sent Helio-dorus to plunder the temple at Jerusalem. Failing he assassinated his master.

11:21 a vile person—Antiochus Epiphanes.

11:22 *also the prince of the covenant*—i.e., the high priest in Israel.

11:23-24 Antiochus Epiphanes in league with Jews and P. Philometer. League broken. War between Epiphanes and Philometer.

11:27 Professed truce Antiochus Epiphanes and P. Philometer.

11:28 *his heart shall be against the holy covenant*— Antiochus Epiphanes defiled the temple when Jerusalem was sacked. See verse 31.

11:30 Popilius Loenus and Roman army forced Antiochus to keep peace. AE the circle! After they left, Antiochus broke his promise and furiously attacked the Jews.

[last part] Antiochus in league with Jewish apostates.

11:31 [last part] 2300 days.

11:32 [last part] The Maccabees.

11:36-38 Isa. 30:33. The last days, antichrist. In the 70th week of ch. 9. The Syrian little horn comes against him. See v. 40. In league with the Roman little horn "The Prince that shall come." The 7 years' covenant.

11:40 A king of the south at the time of the end: but not of Egyptian blood—See Ezek. 30:13; Zech. 10:11.

11:41-42 The Mahometan powers seeking to oust the Jew from Palestine. The king of the north will be unfaithful to his own ally— the king of the south.

11:45 Utter destruction of the last Mahometan ruler—the king of the north.

12:4 Contrast with Revelation—"seal not!"

12:7 *a time, times, and an half*—See this period in the Apocalypse.

12:9 Contrast with the unsealed book of Rev.—ch. 22:10. See Isa. 29:10.

Old Testament -- Hosea – Malachi

Hosea

"A book written for naughty children." Pastor Dolman. Contemporary with Isaiah.

1—3 Division 1—Israel, the unfaithful wife. God's dispensational ways.

1:4 "The blood of Jezreel." The destruction of Ahaz's house in the field of Naboth. Christ's life sworn away—therefore the great tribulation.

1:11 Judah and Israel to be reunited in the land.

2:8 Note the place that knowledge has in this book—2:20; 4:1; 4:6; 5:4; 6:3; 6:6; 8:2; 14:9.

3:3 Me for Himself—Rom. 12:1. Himself for me.

4—14 Division 2—Jehovah's controversy with Israel.

4:1 No truth, no mercy, no knowledge of God.

5:5 Pride goeth before a fall.

5:15 Messiah's return to Heaven—awaiting Israel's repentance.

7:4 The leaven of uncleanness working—See 1 Cor. 5.

7:8 All dough on one side!

10:1 Contrast John 15. See Isa. 5; Rev. 14. Empty lives and empty religion—Isa. 29:8; Matt. 15:9; Jas. 1:26; Isa. 1:13; 1 Cor. 15:2. Empty lives; empty belief; empty religion; empty worship; empty profession.

11:3 Teaching a child to walk. "My safety is not that I take the Lord's hand in mine, but that He takes mine in His—He takes me by the arms." Dolman, [last part] Illustrated in Acts 16:7, 9, 15.

11:8-9 The sovereignty of God in grace. Ch. 13:14.

12:1 "Every wind of doctrine."

12:3-5 Jacob—a supplanter from the first, yet saved by grace.

12:7 The typical Israelite—in his fallen condition.

13:7-8 The nations of the Gentiles. See Dan. 7.

13:9—14:9 Future blessing.

13:11 Prayer answered in judgment.

14:1-3 God Himself supplies the words for the repentant people to use when they return to Him.

Joel

The time of the end—The great tribulation and deliverance of the remnant followed by the establishment of the kingdom on earth. Theme—"The day of the Lord." Joel's date un-known.

A recent locust plague seen as a divine visitation and used as picturing the judgments of the day of the Lord.

1:1 *Joel*—"Jehovah is God."

1:6 The attack of the last Assyrian—the king of the north.

1:7 Israel—the vine and fig tree.

1:14-15 Learn from calamities to humble yourselves before God.

2 The promised outpouring of the Spirit.

2:1-14 The silver trumpets—See Num. 10. The trumpet of alarm.

2:1 "Ye are come to Mount Sion." Note the place that Zion has in Joel. (1) The alarm sounded in Zion.

2:10 See Rev. 6. The sixth seal. Clearly this is symbolical —not literal.

2:13 Call to repentance.

116

2:15 (2) The people called to Zion. See ch. 2:23-31. 2:15-32 The trumpet of the assembling.

2:20 The drying up of the Euphrates. The 6th vial following the 6th trumpet of Revelation.

2:23 (3) Children of Zion—See v. 32.

The latter rain to be restored to Palestine.

2:29 It was the same Spirit poured out on Pentecost— but not the same period of time to which the prophet here refers.

2:32 (4) Deliverance in Zion. The call of God.

3 The premillennial judgments.

3:1-16 (5) Zion the place of judgment.

3:2 The judgment of nations as in Matthew 25.

3:11 The descent of the Lord and the heavenly saints.

3:13 See the harvest and the vintage—Rev. 14.

3:17 (6) Zion God's holy mountain.

3:21 (7) Zion, the end reached.

Amos

The Government of God. His divine sovereignty over Israel and the nations. Somewhat earlier than Isaiah.

1—2 Division 1—Eight messages to the nations surrounding Palestine and to Judah and Israel.

1:1 *Tekoa*—in the Hill country of Judea.

1:9 [last part] i.e., the covenant between Hiram and David.

3—6 Division 2—The Word of the Lord to Israel—the northern kingdom.

3:2 Responsibility flows from acknowledged relationship.

3:6 i.e., Evil in the sense not of sin, but of calamity.

4:6-11 Jehovah's five challenges.

4:12 Warnings unheeded. Judgment must fall.

5:5 A call to turn from false worship.

5:10 The reprover hated. Isa. 29:21.

5:25 The idolatry of the wilderness never judged.

6:12 The fruit of righteousness—See Phil. 1:11, etc.

7—9 Division 3—Five visions having to do with God's sovereignty.

7:10-17 Parenthesis.

7:14 Amos' "call to the ministry."

9:9 Compare the sifting of Peter—Luke 22:31, 32.

Obadiah

Judgment of Edom.

1—15 The character of Edom exposed.
Edom—a type of the flesh characterized by seven things:
(1) Pride v. 3.
(2) Self-confidence v. 3.
(3) Self-exaltation v. 4.
(4) Self-deception vv. 5, 6.
(5) Worldly wisdom v. 8.
(6) Violent opposition to the people of God vv. 10, n.
(7) Gloating over the sufferings of God's people v. 12.

16—21 Israel's deliverance and Edom's final judgment to be coincident or concurrent.

17 It is a great thing when we really possess our possessions, entering into our inheritance in Christ—See Eph. 1:3.

Jonah

118

The Divine Sovereignty.

1:14 [last clause] key verse—*for Thou, O Lord, hast done as it pleased Thee.* See Matt. 12:39; Luke 11:29.

Micah

Contemporary with Isaiah. Cited in Jer. 26:16-19.

Israel's blessing dependent on the coming Saviour.

1—2 Division 1—Arraignment of Israel for their sins.

1:2 As in the beginning of Leviticus: the voice of Jehovah from the sanctuary.

1:11 *Beth-ezel*—The house at hand: that is the inn or half-way house.

1:15 David, the glory of Israel in his day, had sought refuge there.

2:10 The call to separation.

2:11 More ready to listen to false prophets who leave them free to follow their own desires, than to the true man of God who rebukes sin.

3—5 Division 2—Future blessing through Messiah conditioned upon repentance.

3 Princes and priests apostate.

3:5 Teaching for money—"Who when they have something to bite with their teeth, cry Peace; but who prepare war against him that putteth nothing in their mouths." Lesser trans.

3:6 Judicial blindness visited upon the people.

3:8 Empowered by the Holy Spirit. See Acts 1; Zech. 4:6.

4:1-3 Duplicate of Isa. 2:2-4. The first dominion—the Kingdom of God.

4:1 Supreme.

4:2 Universal.

4:3 Peaceful.

4:4-5 Prosperous both in things temporal and things spiritual.

4:8 He who is to rule the nations with the iron rod comes from Israel.

4:10 Rev. 12—when Zion travails.

The Babylonian captivity.

5:1 The smitten judge—Isa. 50:6.

5:2 Christ to be born in Bethlehem.

5:8 This the Jew has been through the centuries of the dispersion, and particularly in these last days.

6 Division 3—The Lord's controversy with His people.

6:5-6 Chastening with a view to blessing.

7 Division 4—Confidence in God—The expression of the remnant in the last days.

7:9 An exercised soul under the discipline of the Lord. See Job 34:31; Heb. 12:5.

Nahum

(Consolation)—The Doom of Nineveh.

"Out of Galilee" Nahum and Jonah both came. Both the Galilean prophets had to do with Nineveh. Nineveh and Babylon both founded by Nimrod.

1 Jehovah the confidence of His people in every time of trouble. Delivered before the death of Sennacherib and therefore a century before the destruction of Nineveh.

1:3 [last part] He is just above the clouds.

1:7 What wondrous contrasts are seen in Him!

1:11 The army of Sennacherib.

2—3 Division 2—The destruction of Nineveh.

2 i.e., The leader of the Babylonians who destroyed Nineveh, entering the city while the people were holding a drunken feast. The river Tigris overflowed and carried away the flood gates, so overwhelming its palaces.

2:11-12 The lion: the king, lioness, and young lions: his household.

3:7 Nineveh literally laid waste as here prophesied.

3:8 *No*—No-Anion destroyed by Sargon shortly before.

3:11 The chastening of the Lord.

3:17 See Rev. 9:7.

3:18 i.e., Saracus grandson of Esar-haddon.

Habakkuk

Possibly a contemporary of Jeremiah. He writes in view of the Chaldean invasion.

1:2 Habakkuk's complaint.

1:5 Jehovah's answer. Cited by Paul, Acts 13:40-41.

1:12 The prophet's expostulation.

2:2 Jehovah's answer.

2:4 The only place "faith" is found in the O.T. In the N.T. it is found in every Book.

The just—Romans.

Shall live—Galatians.

By faith—Hebrews.

2:9 Woe—covetousness—See Heb. 13:5; 1 Tim. 6:8.

2:12 Woe—oppression.

2:15 Woe—sensuality.

2:19 Woe—idolatry.

3 Prayer—In chapter 3 we have "prayer set to music."

3:1 *Shigionoth*—a wandering ode.

3:2 REVIVE Thy Work—Ps. 138:7, Ps. 85:6.

3:4 *horns—or, bright beams out of his side*—where the Roman spear pierced Him!

3:13 See the head that was wounded to death—Rev. 13.

3:16 A sense of utter unworthiness.

Zephaniah

"Hidden of Jehovah."

Written to warn formalists and apostates of coming judgment and to comfort the righteous remnant who cling to the Word of God. Link with the letter to Philadelphia, Revelation 3.

645—610 b.c. Contemporary with Jeremiah.

1 Division 1—Idolaters and apostates must suffer for their sin. The day of the Lord announced.

1:4 The false remnant of Baal. 1:6 Two classes.

1:7 Details of the coming day of wrath.

1:12 Searching out—not in grace but in judgment.

2 The judgment of the nations.

2:1-3 Division 2—The call to repentance. 2:3 Meekness to be sought, see Matt. 11:28-30.

2:4-15 Division 3—The nations in the day of the Lord.

2:10 The pride of Moab.

3 Blessing following judgment.

3:1-7 Division 4—A second call to repentance.

3:2 Four solemn indictments.

3:3-4 Princes, judges, prophets, priests, all apostate.

3:8-20 Division 5—Ultimate salvation.

3:13 The true remnant.

3:14-17 Jehovah "in the midst."

Haggai

[Many passages underlined but no marginal comments.]

Zechariah

The Prophet of the Coming Glory.

Contemporary with Haggai—in the days of the restoration.

Messages to encourage the builders of the house of God.

1:4 A call to consider seriously and turn to the Lord.

1:7—6:15 Eight visions in one night.

1:8-17 Vision 1—Israel guarded by God while in their lowly state.

1:18-21 Vision 2—The four Gentile powers under which they suffered, to be eventually destroyed.

2 Vision 3—Jerusalem to be reclaimed and restored.

2:8 Israel, a missionary people in the last days.

3 Vision 4—The cleansing of the nation.

3:2 Sovereign grace.

3:4-5 Cleansed, clothed, crowned.

4 Vision 5—The filling and anointing with the Spirit.

4:6 The light sustained or maintained by the unseen oil—testimony in the power of the Holy Spirit. See Micah 3:8.

4:10 [last part] Rev. 5:6.

4:14 Kingship or royalty and priesthood.

5:1-4 Vision 6—Iniquity searched out and removed.

"Cursed is everyone that continueth not."

5:5-11 Vision 7—Commercialized religion, Babylonish in origin.

5:7 *talent of lead*—Lead—dross—imitation of silver—base metal—See Ezek. 22:18.

6 Vision 8—Though Israel be surrounded with the mountains of judgment, all shall work for their good.

6:12 The Branch—behold the Man—John 19:5.

6:13 The Royal Priest—"crown Him Lord of all."

7—8 Call to self-judgment in view of the divine purpose of blessing.

8:7-8 The future return of the Jews.

9—14 The prophetic program.

9:9 The First Coming of the Messiah.

9:10 [last part] His Second Coming.

10:1 The latter rain for Israel.

10:11 Connect with Ezek. 30:13.

11 The Good Shepherd rejected: the idol shepherd accepted.

11:15 The antichrist.

12—14 The great tribulation and the deliverance of Judah and Israel, followed by the Kingdom.

14:10 The corner of Hananeel—See Jer. 31:38.

Malachi

Note Jehovah's eightfold controversy with His people.

1:2 Controversy 1—See Rom. 9:13—"Loved" and "hated" have reference here as in Romans 9 to God's dealings with Jacob's descendants and Esau's children in regard to privilege on earth.

1:4 Edom—a type of the flesh—incurably evil.

1:6 Controversy 2.

1:7 Controversy 3.

2:1-2 God's Word to the priests.

2:5 The covenant with Levi.

2:10 Israel, nationally the children of God.

2:14 Controversy 4.

2:15 Warning against mixed marriages.

2:17 Controversy 5.

3:6 The unchanging One.

3:7 Controversy 6.

3:8 Controversy 7.

3:13 Controversy 8.

4:1 Not annihilation—but judgment on earth at the Lord's return.

New Testament -- Matthew – John

Matthew

Christ the King.—The Branch of Jeremiah 23:5.—The Face of a Lion—Ezekiel 1 and Revelation 4.—Christ as the Trespass Offering.—The Gospel for the Jew—proving that Jesus is Messiah.

1:1-17 The genealogy of the King.

The genealogy of Joseph—giving throne rights to Mary's Son—See Luke 3.

1:1-5 Note the story of grace told in the names of the women in the genealogy.

1:11 *Jechonias*—Coniah. A curse rests on Coniah—Christ must come of another line. See Luke 3.

1:18-25 The birth of the King.

1:25 The Virgin Birth—fulfilment of Isa. 7:14.

2 The recognition of the King.

2:2 The first question of the New Testament—See Gen. 3:9.

2:4 The people of the covenant in the right position but the wrong condition.

2:8 Hypocrisy.

2:11 Worship God!—Rev. 22. He is God over all, blessed forever.

Gold—divinity.

Frankincense—perfection of humanity.

Myrrh—death.

3 The consecration and anointing of the King.

3:2 "Kingdom of Heaven" is a dispensational aspect of the Kingdom of God—"the reign of the heavens" upon earth. It is a term used only in Matthew and connects with Daniel 4, "the heavens do rule."

3:10 Not merely to the "fruit" of the tree.

3:15 Pledging Himself to meet every righteous demand of the throne of God on behalf of sinners.

4:1-11 The testing of the King.

4:3 Appeal to the lust of the flesh.

4:5-6 Appeal to the pride of life.

4:8-9 Appeal to the lust of the eye.

4:12-25 The works of the King. His credentials.

5—7 The laws of the King. The royal proclamation. The principles of the Kingdom.

6:9-13 The disciple's prayer.

6:14-15 Mark 11:25, 26—Governmental forgiveness.

7:12 The golden rule—given by Confucius negatively.

8—9 Credentials—the works of the King. Ten signs.

8:11 The Kingdom is Heaven's rule on earth.

8:17 Not vicarious atonement—but sympathy.

8:20 The Son of Man—first instance—used by Jesus of Himself 72 times. For last time see Revelation 14:14.

8:34 Contrast ch. 14:35.

9:37-38 The waiting harvest—Compare John 4:35-38.

10 The heralds of the King.

10:23 An interrupted mission to be resumed after the rapture of the Church.

10:28 The soul lives after the body dies. Both may be lost in Hell. Luke 12:5.

11—12 The rejection of the King.

11:3 The finality of Jesus.

11:22 Differences in judgment according to privileges here.

11:28 *I will give you rest*—only God can do this. It is the same promise Jehovah gave to Moses in Exodus 33:14.

11:29 *My yoke*—He was never under a yoke. He never needed to be restrained, but we do.

12 The authority of the King.

13 The new Aspect of the Kingdom. The mysteries of the Kingdom of Heaven.

13:35 Secret things now revealed. Deut. 29:29.

14—15 The authority and resources of the King. Opposition to the Kingdom.

14:2 The reasoning of a troubled conscience.

14:9 More anxious to keep up appearances than to be right with God.

14:35-36 Note their changed attitude since chapter 8:34.

15:22 As a Gentile she had no claim on "the Son of David."

16 The keys of the Kingdom—the first mention of the Church. Jesus foretells His death for the first time—v. 21. He foretells His Second Coming for the first time—v. 27.

He tells of His Church for the first time—v. 18.

16:6-12 Leaven—always evil. Leaven of the Pharisees, hypocrisy—self-righteousness.

Leaven of the Sadducees, doctrinal error—materialism—rationalism.

6:18 The Living Stone—1 Pet. 2:4.

17 The glory of the King—a picture of the coming Kingdom.

17:2 The glory of God in the face of Christ Jesus—2 Cor. 4.

18 Instruction as to discipline in the Church.

18:19 *agree*—symphonize—to be in complete harmony with God and with each other.

18:23-35 Governmental forgiveness which may be revoked if there be inconsistency.

19—20 The last journey of the King—Going up to Jerusalem to die.

19:8 Christ sets His O.K. upon the Genesis account of the beginning of the human race.

19:17 The test: He is God or he is not good!

19:21 A call to recognize the lordship of Christ.

19:28 Regeneration—only twice used in the Bible—See Titus 3:5.

20:1-16 Reward is according to opportunities embraced —not merely the amount of work performed.

21 The triumphal entry of the King.

21:22 The prayer of faith.

22—25 The teaching of the King. 2:16 What vile hypocrisy!

24—25 The second Sermon on the Mount. The King's prophetic discourse.

26 The agony of the King.

26:7-9 The flesh cannot understand heart-appreciation of Jesus.

26:14 The depravity of the flesh seen in Judas.

26:15 *thirty pieces of silver*—the price of a slave or a common ox.

26:35 The confidence of the flesh.

26:51 The forwardness of the flesh.

26:61 Utter perversion of His words.

26:70 The breakdown of the flesh.

27 The crucifixion of the King.

27:3 The remorse of the flesh.

27:9 Zechariah was probably in the roll that began with Jeremiah.

27:24 *washed his hands*—"Crucified under Pontius Pilate."

27:50 *yielded up the ghost*—dismissed His Spirit. "When He willed to die, He died as He willed." F. E. Marsh.

28 The Resurrection of the King.

28:19 [last part] The Holy Trinity—Isa. 48:16.

28:19-20 Going...

teach—Disciple...

Baptizing...

Teaching...

Disciple is the emphatic word.

Mark

Behold My Servant!

The Branch of Zechariah 3:8.

The Face of an Ox. Ezekiel 1.

Christ as the Sin Offering. Leviticus 5.

1:1-13 The Servant introduced. No geneology.

1:14—3:35 His early ministry.

1:23-26 His power over demons.

1:30-31 His power over disease.

Fever—the power of sin.

1:40-41 Leprosy—the uncleanness of sin.

2:3-12 Palsy—the helplessness of the sinner.

2:22 The new wine of the gospel is not to be put into the old legal forms.

2:28 His authority, though in servant guise.

3:22 Blasphemy against the Holy Spirit.

3:28-29 Sin against Him as Man pardonable—but to reject Him as God is fatal.

3:31-34 The new relationship.

4—9 Teaching and working.

4:13 This is the foundation parable.

5:4 Society restrains—Jesus liberates.

5 Three pictures:

The man—desperate sinners controlled by furious passions—

dominated by satanic power.

The women—timid and anxious souls groping after light and help.

The child—people dead spiritually to be awakened to life by the gospel.

5:24-27 Many who thronged Him; few who touched Him in faith.

6:5 Limited by unbelief.

6:16 The voice of an accusing conscience.

7 A new doctrine of defilement.

7:6-7 Voiding the Word of God by human tradition.

7:21-23 The weeds that grow in the natural heart.

8:15 Matt. 16:6—*leaven*: symbol of evil.—*leaven of the Pharisees* —hypocrisy.—*leaven of Herod*—worldliness. See 1 Cor. 5.

8:35 "God harden me against myself
This coward with pathetic voice;
Who craves for ease, and rest, and joys." Christina Rosetti.

9 The Kingdom in embryo.

9:15 Was the glory still shining in His face?

10:45 The Servant of God and Man.

11:25 Conditions of answered prayer.

14:4 The flesh cannot appreciate what is done only for love of Jesus.

15:28 "He who knew no sin."

15:33 "Made sin."

16 The Servant exalted—His Resurrection.

16:2 The first Lord's Day.

Luke

Christ as Son of Man.—
The Branch of Zechariah 6:12.—
The Face of a Man, Ezekiel 1.—
Christ as the Peace Offering, Leviticus 3.
Outline:
(1) 1—3—The introduction.
(2) 4—9:50—From the temptation to the Transfiguration.
(3) 9.51—21:38—The last six months of Ministry.
(4) 22—24—Closing scenes and the Resurrection.

1:10 The fellowship of prayer.

1:20-22 Unbelief sealed his lips. See v. 64.

Dumb lips tell of an unbelieving heart. Rom. 10:9, 10.

1:27 A Virgin in polluted Nazareth!

1:35 He who was ever God the Son becomes in grace the Son of God as Man born of a Virgin.

1:64 Faith opened his mouth.

2:24 The offering of the poor.

2:38 [last part] The godly remnant.

2:46 Jesus in the midst—See John 19:18.

3:1 Note the definiteness of the dates.

3:21 Note the place given to prayer in the life of the Son of Man, as related by Luke. See ch. 5:16.

3:27 *Zorobabel—Salathiel*—Note that the lines intertwine here.

4:1-13 Moral order of the temptations—"The lust of the flesh" v. 3; "The lust of the eye" v. 5; "The pride of life" v. 9.

4:10-11 Omitting what was vitally important.

4:20 *He closed the book,*—He puts the entire dispensation of grace into a comma!

5:16 Prayer—See ch. 6:12.

5:21 And here was God in their midst, and they knew Him not!

5:29 "The table talk of the Son of Man."

The feast in the house of Levi. See Ch. 7:36.

6:1 In Greek—"the second first"—i.e., the second after the feast of firstfruits.

6:11 *filled with madness*—angered by His grace!

6:12 Prayer. See ch. 9:18.

6:31 The "golden rule."

6:42 *beam*—i.e., a large splinter—as in the everyday language of the common people. Confirmed by the papyri.

7:29 God justified as they received His sentence against themselves.

7:36-50 The table talk of the Son of Man in the Pharisee's house. See ch. 10:38.

8:10 The Kingdom of God is moral. In Matt. 13 it is "the Kingdom of Heaven" which is dispensational—the form the Kingdom takes during a given age.

8:11 [last part] "The devil knows that men will be saved if they believe!" A.H.S.

8:44 The blue border.

9:18 Prayer—See ch. 9:28.

9:28 Prayer—See ch. 11:1.

10:2 The waiting harvest—See John 4:35.

10:38-42 The table talk of the Son of Man—with Mary and Martha. See ch. 11:37.

10:42 [first part] "Of one thing there is need."

11:1 Prayer—See ch. 22:41.

11:20 Ex. 8:19 The finger of God is the Spirit of God. Matt. 12:28.

11:31-32 Solomon typical of Christ as the wisdom of God, Jonah as the one who went into death and rose again.

11:37-54 The table talk of the Son of Man—in another Pharisee's house. See ch. 14:1.

11:44 Defiling when men do not realize it. See Num. 19.

12 Prophetic testimony—The Great Preacher, leaven— always symbolic of evil. See 1 Cor. 5.

12:5 Matt. 10:28—The soul immortal.

12:50 The baptism of wrath upon the Cross.

13:6 The fig tree: Israel nationally.

14:1 The table talk of the Son of Man in the house of a chief Pharisee. See ch. 19:5.

14:14 [last phrase] The first Resurrection.

15:4-7 The seeking Saviour—The lost sheep.

15:7 Saints in heaven rejoice when souls are saved!

15:8-10 The Holy Spirit's work—The lost coin.

15:11-24 The Father's love—The lost son.

15:25-32 The elder son—"Not lost or not saved." The self-righteous.

16:7 i.e., He made himself responsible for the difference.

16:23 *hell*—Hades—the abode of unclothed spirits.

16:27-31 Six brothers: one in hell and five on the way!

17:11-19 The ten lepers—See Lev. 13.

18:9-14 The only two religions.

18:19 He is either God or He is not good.

19:3 [last clause] A man who had "come short."

19:5 The table talk of the Son of Man in the house of Zacchaeus. Conversation on the way to his home. See ch. 22:13.

20:4 It was at John's baptism He was anointed as the Prophet, Priest, and King. There the Father's voice and the descending sign accredited Him.

20:35 The first resurrection.

21:24 [last clause] See Ezek. 30:3—"The time of the heathen."

21:25 *distress of nations, with perplexity*—"crowding pressure of nations with no way out."

21:29 Judah—fig tree. The Gentile nations of the prophetic earth. The Fig Tree: Patriarchs firstripe of the fig tree—Hos. 9:10. See Joel 1:7; Jer. 24:1-10; 29:17; Luke 13:6-9; Matt. 21:18-20; Hos. 14:8; Isa. 27:6; Mic. 4:4; Jno. 1:47-51.

21:35 Them that dwell on the earth—see this class in Revelation.

22:2 Religious bigotry allied with treachery and covetousness.

22:10-11 The ministry of the Word—the water of life— leads to the place of communion.

22:13 The table talk of the Son of Man. The last Passover and the Lord's Supper.

22:24 At such a time!

22:31 In Satan's sieve. See Amos 9:9.

22:32 Advocacy even before the open failure.

22:33 The confidence of the flesh.

22:45 Peter was sleeping when he should have been praying. The slothfulness of the flesh.

22:50 Peter acts in the energy of the flesh.

22:54 The backwardness of the flesh.

22:55 Seeking comfort among the enemies of Christ.

22:57-60 The denial.

22:61 The beginning of Peter's restoration was that look of love.

23:8 It was not because he desired to know Christ as Saviour—but to satisfy the craving for wonders.

23:25 The end of man's free will.

24:19-21 They believed in and loved Him still but hope had fled.

24:25-36 Three lines of ministry: by the way—in the home—in the upper room.

24:25 Note the rebuke for not believing all that the prophets had spoken.

24:30 He became the Host!

24:31 Their eyes opened. See v. 32.

24:32 Opened the Scriptures. See v. 45.

24:45 Ps. 119:73—Opened their understanding.

24:51 See Acts 1—"He was taken up."

John

Christ as the Eternal Son—
The Branch of Isaiah 4:2-5.—
The Face of an Eagle, Ezek. 1.

1:1 [first part] When everything that had beginning began, the Word was.
In the beginning was the Word—eternity of being.
the Word was with God—distinct personality.
the Word was God—full deity.

1:2 Eternal Son.

1:3 Creator.

1:4 [first part] Source of life.

[last part] Source of light.

1:12 sons—children, born ones.

138

1:30 before—Christ's preexistence before John the Baptist. See ch. 8:58.

2:6-10 Empty Jewish ceremonies filled with the water of the Word produce rich wine of truth.

3:16 For God so loved the world—the lake. that He gave His only begotten Son—the river. that whosoever believeth in Him—the pitcher. should not perish but have everlasting life—the draught.

4:7 Note His method of approach to a sinner's heart.

4:10 living water—The gospel message in the power of the Holy Spirit—See ch. 3:5.

4:14 "Whatever water means here it must mean the same in John 3."

4:16 Grappling with conscience. 4:34 Oh, to be more like Him!

4:35 The waiting harvest. Compare Matt. 9:37, 38; Luke 10:2.

5:1-9 In John, the feasts are "of the Jews" not "of Jehovah" for the Christ of God who is the antitype of all is seen as rejected from the very start. At Bethesda there was help for the strongest and best. In the gospel there is salvation for the weakest and the worst.

5:17 Jesus asserts His perfect equality with the Father.

5:19 So intimate are the relations of the Persons in the Godhead that neither can do anything without the other.

5:32-39 Fourfold witness:
v. 33—John—See ch. 10:3.
v. 36—The works He did—See ch. 10:25.
v. 37—The Father—See ch. 8:13-18.
v. 39—The Scriptures—See v. 46.

5:43 Antichrist—the wilful king of Daniel 11.

The man of sin of 2 Thessalonians 2.

5:47 The Lord authenticates the Mosaic authorship of the Pentateuch.

6:3 A scene of communion. We do not read that a word was said. It was hallowed fellowship. He loves thus to "sit" with His own.

6:27 The "sealed" Bread of God for hungry men!

6:40 God the Father's will and the believer's salvation bound up together.

7:23 Referring to the man healed at Bethesda, on His previous visit—ch. 5.

7:52 Overlooking Nahum and Jonah.

8:9 The Light of the world—exposing the hypocrisy of the accusers of the woman.

8:16 Who but God the Son could rightfully say, "I and the Father."

8:41 A slur at the Virgin birth. 8:44 Slanders God to man and man to God.

Satan—adversary.

Devil—diabolous—slanderer.

> An apostate—"Abode not in the truth."
> Lucifer's fall—Isa. 14:12; Ezek. 28:11.
> His activity—Gen. 3 to Rev. 20.
> His doom—Rev. 20.
> A deceiver—liar—no truth in him.
> A manslayer—ruining men to spite God.

8:59 The stones that were for the adultress before, now are for Him!

9 From blindness and beggary to worship. 9:2 The Pharisees taught that a man could sin in the womb, basing it on the words, "He took his brother by the heel in the womb."

9:34 Men are born in sin—not in sins.

10:1-3 Judaism was the sheepfold, Christ the Good Shepherd entered in by the door. John the Baptist, the porter.

10:11 Why Christ died. The Person who laid down His life. What He was gave the value to what He did.

10:15-18 Five P's:
Person who died—v. 15.
Persons for whom He died—v. 15.
Price He paid—v. 17.
Principle on which He acted—v. 18a.
Power behind the action—v. 18b.

10:27 Marks of the sheep of Christ:
1—hear His voice.
2—follow Him.

11—12 The witness of the Father to Jesus.

11:25-26 i.e., In the hour when He is to be so manifested!

11:44 Life but not liberty.

12:1 New life.

12:2 Service, communion.

12:3 Worship.

12:28 i.e., glorified in the resurrection of Lazarus. He would glorify it in Christ's resurrection also.

13:23, 25 *leaning and lying*—Note the two different words. *lying*—"falling back on."

3:36 The proper beginning of chapter 14.

whither goest thou?—The answer is found in chapter 14:2.

4:2 *mansions*—abiding places. "If it were not so would I have told you I go to prepare a place for you?"

4:16 *I will pray the Father*—to ask as a demand, in one's own right.

4:16, 26 *Comforter*—"He dwelleth with you." The Holy Spirit before Pentecost. Striving with the Antediluvians: Gen. 6:3; 1 Pet. 3:18-20. Angelic ministry prominent in patriarchal days—Gen. 10—50. The Holy Spirit the author of the Scriptures—1 Pet. 1:11; 2 Pet. 1:20; 2 Sam. 23:2; Neh. 9:30. In the wilderness—Neh. 9:20. Men empowered for testimony and service—Bezaleel and Aholiab—Ex. 31:3; 35:30-35. Balaam—Samson— Gideon—Saul—David—etc., etc.—John the Baptist. The promise to give to those who ask— Luke 11:13.

14:27 Peace I leave—Peace with God. He left this when He died. He gives peace—as the living One.

14:31 The burnt offering.

15:1 The true Vine—in contrast to Israel, the empty vine—Hos. 10:1; Isa. 5, etc.; Ps. 80:8; Rev. 14:17.

15:3 Cleansing by the Word. See ch. 13.

15:4-7 "Abiding in Christ and abounding for Christ." The soul's need:
Pure air—prayer.

Good food—the Word of God.

Constant exercise—obedience to God.

Connect John 15:4; 15:10; Col. 4:2; 1 Cor. 15:58; Ps. 84:7.

15:7 The secret of prevailing prayer.

16:1-16 The personality of the Holy Spirit. One with the Father and the Son: the Holy Trinity. Matt. 28:19; Gen. 1:1; Isa. 48:16; Luke 3:22; 2 Cor. 13:1. Personality attributed to Him. He may be grieved— Eph. 4:30; insulted—Heb. 10:29; He guides, speaks, convinces (see vv. 8-13); knows—1 Cor. 2:11; searches out and reveals—v. 10; teaches—v. 12; controls and distributes the gifts—1 Cor. 12. 16:23 His name on a check is good for any amount.

To the Bank of Heaven

Pay to *whosoever* abides in Me *whatsoever* he shall ask. —Jesus Christ

17 The High Priest in intercession.

18:4 The Eternal Son!

18:8 The gospel illustrated.

18:10 The energy of the flesh.

18:18 Warming himself at the world's fire.

18:28 So careful of the ritual, so careless of the life of the Saviour!

18:36 His Kingdom heavenly in origin—but eventually to be set up on earth.

19:2 thorns—the fruit of the curse. See Gen. 3:18.

19:18 Luke 2:46. Jesus in the midst. See Matt. 18:20.

19:20 Hebrew, Greek, Latin—law, culture, and religion.

19:34, 35 Witnesses of the death: the finished work of Christ. See 1 John 1:6, etc.

19:39 The burial of a King. They laid Him on a bed of spices.

20:17 My brethren: new creation relationship—the fruit of His death.

20:22 The last Adam: a quickening Spirit.

Acts

1:8 Power: "It is not skillfully composed discourse, nor the mode of delivery, nor well-practised eloquence that produces conviction, but the communication of divine power."—From Origen (*Commentary on John's Gospel*)

1:22 The last official act of the old dispensation.

2:1 The new dispensation of the grace of God ushered in.

2:14 Filled, baptized, sealed, and anointed all at the same time. Filled—See ch. 4:8.

2:16 this is that—the same in kind—but not the times of Joel 2.

3:17 *through ignorance*—A city of refuge opened to them.

3:24 [last clause] i.e., the days of the Messiah.

4:11 The rejected Stone—Matt. 21:42, Ps. 118:22.

5:15 Shadow ministry—Peter walked in the sunlight of God's love and so his very shadow was full of blessing.

"It is no hard work to cast a shadow, it is simply living in the sunlight." Dr. A.T.S.

"You can't dispute with a shadow." It is the life that counts when perhaps the one who casts the shadow is quite unconscious of it.

5:33 *they were cut to the heart*—"they were infuriated."

6:3, 5 Full—a normal condition. See ch. 7:55.

7:2-3 Led by the God of glory up to the glory of God. See v. 55.

8:29 *join thyself*—literally, "glue thyself."

8:37 Verse 37 omitted in most mss. But we have here proof positive that in the early church confession of faith in Christ preceded baptism.

10:2 Evidently a quickened soul—a proselyte from the Gentiles.

10:38 Jesus anointed by the Spirit as Prophet, Priest, and King.

11:23 Purpose of heart—2 Tim. 3:10; Dan. 1:8.

11:25 Evidently Paul's sojourn in Arabia was just prior to this (?).

13—14 Paul's first missionary journey.

13:9 From this time the apostle is called Paul.

14:1 so spake—It is possible so to speak that no one will believe.

14:28 End of the first mission to the Gentiles.

15:1 Adding to the work of Christ.

15:26 *hazarded*—literally—"delivered up"—same as in Galatians 114—"gave" Himself. Eph. 5:2, 25.

15:36 Inception of the second missionary journey.

15:40 Beginning of the journey.

16 Guidance:
(1) By hearing—v. 6.
(2) By the hand or feeling—v. 7.
(3) Vision—by sight—v. 9.
(4) Guidance by discernment—v. 15.

16:10 Luke joins the party at Troas.

16:12 i.e., A Roman colonia—having the standing of the imperial city itself.

17:6 The world was wrong side up ever since the fall of man.

17:27 *feel*—only place in the New Testament.

17:31 The Day of Judgment—Heb. 9:27; Psalm 9:8.

18:12, 17 *Gallio*—the indifferent.

18:22 End of the second mission.

18:23 The third missionary journey.

18:24-28 Apollos:
1—A man of great natural endowments.
2—A man of learning.
3—Mighty in the Scriptures.
4—Zealous.
5—Limited knowledge of the Lord Jesus.
6—Confined his preaching to what he knew.
7—Willing to learn from less gifted people.
8—Knew how to use knowledge aright.

19:1 N.B.—Not a Christian company—simply Jewish disciples of John the Baptist.

19:2 [first part] Did you, upon believing, receive the Holy Spirit? literal translation.

19:15 Demons know Him—Mark 5:7.

20:26 Compare Ezek. 33.

20:35 [last part] was wont to say. It was a characteristic habit of His, though nowhere recorded in the Gospels.

21:4 Note that the Holy Spirit seems distinctly to warn Paul not to go to Jerusalem. It is very evident however that Paul did *not* recognize this. There is no hint of self-will on his part.

21:11 The second warning—but not a command this time.

21:23 Was not this a trap, an effort to have Paul compromise the truth for the sake of peace?

21:26 And this in the face of the truth of Hebrews 9 and 10.

23:27 *having understood*—a prevarication.

24:25 Felix, the procrastinator.

24:26 Covetous and adulterous.

25:3 Hypocrisy of religious leaders.

25:18 Festus the scorner.

25:19-20 To Festus these were most trivial matters!

26:9 Conscience not a safe guide. It must be instructed by revelation. See ch. 23:1.

26:10 *voice*—vote. Saul was evidently a member of the Sanhedrin.

26:26 Agrippa—the almost persuaded.

26:28 "With how little wouldst thou persuade me."

26:29 *both almost, and altogether*—"Whether by little or by much."

27:24 How blessed to be Sailing with Paul!

27:25 Divine sovereignty—See v. 31.

27:31 Human responsibility.

Romans

The Epistle of the Forum.—Note the large use of legal terms. Theme: "The Righteousness of God."

Part 1 1—8—Doctrinal—"The Righteousness of God revealed in the gospel."

Division 1 1—5:11—God's way of dealing with our sins. Section 1 1—3:20—The need of the gospel.

1:1-7 Sub-sec. 1—Salutation.

The key in verse one—"gospel."

1:3 Humanity of our Lord.

1:4 Deity of our Lord.

1:8-17 Sub-sec. 2—Introduction.

1:9 Acts 27:23—Service.

1:10 See Acts 27, 28 for the answer.

1:17 i.e., faithwise—not of works.

1:18-32 Sub-sec. 3—The barbarian's condition.

1:20 things that are made—"poem"—See Eph. 2:10.

2—3:20 Sub-sec. 4—The cultured Gentile's condition. The moralist.

2:22 [last part] to buy and sell idols.

3 The summing up.

3:9 The great indictment.

3:21—5:11 The gospel in relation to sins.

3:24 *freely*—Dorion: same word is translated "without-a-cause" in John 15:25.

3:31 The law is not discredited, but its righteousness is fully recognized in the gospel.

4:4 Reward is for works; justification is by grace. See Heb. 10:35.

4:5 God justifies the ungodly who believe in Christ who died for the ungodly—See ch. 5:6.

4:15 The law gives sin the specific character of transgression.

5:1 Note the 3 "therefores":

5:1—"Justification."
8:1—"Sanctification."
12:1—"Consecration."

5:10-11 Reconciled to God by the death of Christ. Col. 1:21.

5:10-11 God received the atonement and we the reconciliation.

5:12—8:39 The gospel in relation to sin.

5:14 *death*—King. Note the five kings.

5:17 Believers—kings.

Transferred—from Adam to Christ.

Transformed—into the Spirit of Christ.

Translated—at the Coming of Christ.

5:21 Sin—king.

Grace—king.
Christ—king.

6:11 *Reckon!*

6:13 *Yield!* See 2 Chron. 30:8.

6:16 *Obey!* (George Matheson's poem, "Make me a captive, Lord," was pasted in Dr. Ironside's Bible beside this verse. It appears in full in the poetry section in front.)

7 The two husbands.

7:1 Death severs relationship to law.

7:4 Christ's death to law was my death to that principle.

7:7 The old husband not to be confounded with the old master (Pharaoh).

8:2 The Spirit's law: life in Christ Jesus.

8:9 Sealing with the Spirit.

8:16 The Spirit bearing witness. See Heb. 10 and 1 John 5-

8:29 Note: Foreordination is not to salvation—but to Christ-conformity.
Part 2 9—11—Dispensational—The Righteousness of God in harmony with His dispensational ways.

All Israel's past blessings depended upon sovereign electing grace.

9 God's *past* dealings with Israel.

An elect nation cannot rightfully call in question God's electing grace as applied to the Gentiles in this age.

9:2 Great heaviness and continual sorrow are not inconsistent with fullness of joy in the Lord.

9:6 Note—the theme here is that of a place of special privilege on earth.

9:22 Why object to God's present work of grace when the Jew had rejected the mercy shown him?

10 God's present dealings with Israel.

11 God's future dealings with Israel.

11:11-12 The calling of the Gentiles—See Isaiah 49.

11:16-26 The olive tree—The natural branches torn out. See Jer. 11:16.

11:25 The mystery of the olive tree.

Part 3 12—16—Practical—The Righteousness of God apprehended produces practical righteousness in us.

12:1 A living sacrifice—See Num. 8:11-21; Dan. 3:28; Acts 15:26. Exhortation based on chapters 1—8.

12:2 The free service of a willing mind as a result of the new life.

12:3 Responsibility toward brethren in Christ generally.

12:4-5 The One Body—1 Cor. 12.

12:18-21 Belongs to the next chapter.

13 Responsibility toward governments and men of the world.

13:14 Augustine's conversion.

14:1—15:7 Responsibility to walk charitably toward weaker brethren.

"First. Is it lawful? May I do it and not sin? Second. Is it becoming in me as a Christian? May I do it and not wrong my profession? Third. Is it expedient? May I do it and not offend my weak brothers?" —Bernard of Clairvaux.

15:13 believing what?—Man's ruin—1—3:20. God's remedy 3:21—5:11. In a new race with a new head—5:12-21. Dead to the sin within—ch. 6. Dead to law— ch. 7. In Christ—Christ in us, God for us—ch. 8.

15:29 Yet he came bound with a chain after being twice shipwrecked.

16:1-24 Salutations.

16:25-27 Appendix—the mystery.

16:26 the scriptures of the prophets—"prophetic writings," i.e., of the N.T.

1 Corinthians

The Church of God and its Order.

1:10 The unity of the Church.

1:17 Message of the Church.

2:2 "A Christless Cross no refuge is for me,
A Crossless Christ my Saviour might not be,
But, O Christ Crucified, I rest in Thee."

2:11 Personality of the human spirit.

3 The work of the Church.

4 Ministry of the Church.

4:6 Literally, I have used Apollos and myself as illustrations for your sakes that ye might learn in us (the meaning of) nothing beyond what is written.

5 Discipline of the Church.

5:6 The leaven—See Hos. 7:4.

6—10 Social life of the Church.

6:13-20 Note how the Holy Trinity is interested in the believer's body.
The Lord for the body. The body indwelt by the Holy Spirit. Glorify God in your body. Rom. 12:1.

7:6 i.e.,—he permits but does not command the advice of verse 5.

8:2 See Jas. 1:5.

9:26-27 "I am a boxer, who does not inflict blows upon the air, but I hit hard and straight at my own body." Weymouth's translation.

10:11 Note four views of the Scriptures:
1. Literal—*all these things happened.*
2. Typical—*unto them for ensamples.*
3. Spiritual—*written for our admonition.*
4. Dispensational—*upon whom the ends of the world (ages) are come.*

10:32 The threefold division of mankind.

11—14 Meetings of the Church.

12 Note: The "Body" here is the aggregate of believers on the earth at a given time. In Ephesians it is all from Pentecost to the Lord's return.

12:4-6 The Trinity.

12:12 The human body.

12:13 The Body of Christ.
Baptized in the Spirit:
See the promise through John—Matt. 3:11; Mark 1:8; Luke
3:16; John 1:31.
The promise of the Lord—Acts 1:5-8.
The promise of the Father—Luke 1:49; Isa. 49:3; Joel 2:2; Ezek.
37:26.
The Promise fulfilled:
Israel—Acts 2:1-7.
Samaria—Acts 8:14-17.
Gentiles—Acts 10:44-48; Acts 11:15, 16.
John's disciples—Acts 19:1-6.

15 The confidence and hope of the Church.

15:3 The death of Christ:
1—Voluntary—John 10.
2—The purpose for which He became Incarnate— Heb. 2.
3—Substitutionary.
4—To reconcile to God.
5—Ends our relationship with the old creation.
Dead to sin—the world—law.

15:24-26 The mediatorial kingdom to be delivered up to the
Father—The work of the Son—as receiver of the fallen universe—
completed.

15:28 [last clause] i.e., God—the eternal Trinity, Father, Son, and
Holy Spirit.

15:36 Fool—not implying lack of intelligence—but one who makes
a bad use of it. Not *moros* as in Matthew

5:22 but *aphron*, heedless. 15:39 No evolution of species.

15:44 *natural*—psychical; *spiritual*—pneumatical.

15:52 "In a moment"—See Job 21:13.

15:58 The Lord's Return—the incentive to service. See 1 Thess.
1:9, 10.

16 Concluding exhortations and salutations.

2 Corinthians

1:10 Threefold deliverance. See Ps. 116:8.

1:14 [last part] i.e., at the judgment seat of Christ. See Phil. 1:6.

1:21-22 The operations of the Spirit of God.

2:3-5 Note how frequently he uses "you all" in Philippians, as also here.

4:8-9 "Without a way but not without a by-way." Emph. Bible.

> 4:16-18 Note the contrasts:
> Outward man—inward man.
> Perish—renewed.
> Light—weight.
> Affliction—glory.
> Moment—eternal.
> Things seen—unseen.
> Temporal—eternal.
> Continue in chapter 5—contrasts throughout.

4:16 The outward man—the body.

The inward man—the spirit and soul.

5:6 Gal. 2:20—Is the body all?—See 2 Cor. 12:3.

5:19 The ministry of reconciliation—John 3:17; Deut. 20:10.

> 5:21 The basis of reconciliation. The sin offering. We are now made, in Christ, the display of divine righteousness.
> The Sinless One made sin.
> Knew no sin:
> 1—Never sinned.
> 2—No sin within.
> 3—Incapable of sin, impeccable.
> Made sin:
> 1—No change in Him.

2—No change in the Father's love.
3—Bore divine judgment as sin offering.
Result: We—sinners—made the display of divine righteousness in Him. Phil. 3.
He did no sin—1 Pet. 2:22.
"In Him is no sin."—1 John 3:5.
Tempted apart from sin—Heb. 4:15.

6 Ambassadors for Christ:
1—Their authority.
2—Qualifications.
3—Message.
4—Recall.

6:3 A blameless ministry.

6:4 The minister's credentials.

6:6 The minister's character.

6:7-10 The minister's contrasts.

8:3 Willing beyond their ability.

8:4 [last phrase] Fellowship of serving by giving.

8:9 "When was He rich?"

9:8-11 "From God to God." He the source of all blessing which in turn leads the heart out in worship and praise to Him—See Eccl. 1:7.

10:4 Eph. 6:11-13—The Christian warfare.

10:7 *outward appearance*—1 Sam. 16:7.

11:2 The Church the espoused bride.

11:19 Keen irony.

12:2 Consciousness out of the body taken for granted.

12:8 Prayer to Christ, as to the Father.

13:14 *communion*—Fellowship, partnership, companionship. "to eat bread together"—Latin. Together—breadship.

Galatians

Law and Grace.

1—2 Personal.

1:1-5 Salutation. 1:6-10 Introduction.

1:11-23 Paul's conversion and call to the apostolate.

1:13 *conversation*—behavior.

2:11 Controversy with Peter.

2:20 The Cross—See Rom. 6:6.

3—4 Doctrinal.

3:27 See Col. 2:12; Rom. 6:3, 4.

5—6 Practical.

5:15 Dogs!

6:14 The Cross. See ch. 2:20. See the type in Numbers 19:6. Cicero wrote: "Far be the very name of a cross, not only from the bodies of Roman citizens, but from their imaginations, eyes, and ears."

6:17 "I bear branded in my body the stigmata of the Lord Jesus."

Ephesians

The N.T. Book of Joshua.—The Body of Christ.— The Heavenlies our present portion.

1:4 *according to*—See Esther 2:18.

1:17-18 Prayer for knowledge. Paul's first prayer   See ch. 3:14.

1:22 *all*—i.e., all principalities, powers, etc.

2:10 *workmanship*—"poem"—See Rom. 1:20.

2:17 *which were afar off*—Gentiles.

that were nigh—Jews.

3:3 *the mystery*—Col. 1:26. 3:8 See v. 16.

3:10 Angels learning the wisdom of God in us.

3:11 "Purpose of the ages."

3:14 Prayer for power.

3:16 *according to*—not "out of" but "according to." riches—1—Endowment.
"Glory is the excellence of anything in display." Alex. Stewart of Glasgow, quoted by F. E. Marsh, strengthened with might—2—Enduement—power or ability.

<blockquote>
3:17 [first part] 3—Enthronement.
[last part] 4—Environment.
rooted—like a tree.
grounded—like a building.
</blockquote>

3:18 Four dimensions—spiritual knowledge of the divine purpose. comprehend—5—Enlightenment.

3:19 6—Enrichment.

3:20 Compare with Jude 24 and Rom. 16:25.

[last part] 7—Empowerment or equipment.

4:8 Captivity captive explained in Isa. 14:2. See Judges 5:12.

4:12 Omit the commas.

4:20 Christ glorified directs our attention to Jesus as He was here on earth.

4:24 A new order of man—See Col. 3:10 where a different word is used.

4:30 The Holy Spirit—a divine person, who may be:
Vexed—Isa. 63:10.
Resisted—Acts 7:51.
Grieved—Eph. 4:30.
Quenched—1 Thess. 5:19.

5:2 The Burnt Offering—Lev. 1; Ps. 40.

5:9 Fruit of the Spirit—Gal. 5:22—Some read "Fruit of the Light."

5:14 [last clause] or "Christ shall shine upon thee."

5:18 Filled with the Spirit—Compare Col. 3:16.

See Acts 2:4; 4:8; 4:31; 6:3,5; 7:55; 9:17; 11:24; 13:9; 13:52. Full of the Holy Spirit—the normal condition of one who is walking with God. Filled— special filling for special occasions.

5:15 Contrast with the shoes of Joab—1 Kings 2:5.

Philippians

Christian Experience: Christ in Life and Death.
Key words: Mind, Gospel.
"The dear Lord's best interpreters
Are humble, human souls.
The gospel of a life like theirs
Is more than creeds or scrolls."

1 Christ, the believer's Life.

1:6 2 Cor. 1:14—i.e., the judgment seat of Christ. See v. 10.

1:9 judgment—"keen perception."

1:11 Amos 6:12—fruits of righteousness—See Heb. 12:11; Jas. 3:17, 18.

1:12-26 Personal.

1:27-30 Exhortation.

1:27 *striving together*—co-operating vigorously.

2 Christ our Example—"Others."

3 Christ the believer's Object.

3:2-4 Deliverance from confidence in the flesh and the religion of the flesh. Paul's Personal Experience.

3:5 *Benjamin*—A son of the free wife—not a bondmaid.

3:9 Contrast Deut. 6:25.

3:11 "The out-resurrection from among."

3:13 *one thing*—Ps. 27:4; Luke 10:42.

3:15 *perfect*—mature.

3:20 *our conversation*—our citizenship and hope. *Politeuma*—commonwealth, citizenship, politics.

4 Christ our Strength.

Colossians

The Headship of Christ.

Note the place the "will of God" has in this letter.

Probably written A.D. 63.

1 The Pre-Eminent One.

1:4-5 Faith, hope, and love—1 Cor. 13. Note the order here is changed. 1 Thess. 1:3.

1:9-11 Prayer—seven petitions.

1:9 True knowledge.

> 1:10 *Walk worthy*:
> Of your calling—Eph. 4:1.
> Of the gospel—Phil. 1:27.
> Of the Lord—Col. 1:16.

1:11 Divine strength.

1:12-14 Thanksgiving.

1:15-19 The First Begotten.

1:15 Firstborn—not necessarily the one born first—but a title of dignity. See Deut. 21:16;Ps. 89:25-27. Christ —greater than creation—not a part of it.

Firstborn of all creation—See v. 18.

Exact image—not a distant eon.

1:17 before—See John 1:17; John 8:58. Christ's pre-existance. "What makes gravitation gravitate?" Christ!

1:18 *firstborn from the dead*—Rom. 8:29.

1:19 In Him all the fullness was pleased to dwell.

1:20-22 Twofold reconciliation.

Sin had ruptured the condition of concord or conciliation between man and God. Christ has wrought the re-conciliation. See Rom. 5:10-11; 2 Cor. 5:18-21; Eph. 2:10-17.

1:23-29 Twofold ministry.

1:23 *If ye continue*—the test of profession.

made a minister—a minister of the gospel.

1:25 A minister of the Church

2 Our union with the Head. Complete in Him.

2:2 *full assurance*—See Heb. 6:11.

2:4-7 Our link with Him.

2:4 Christ the Antidote for every fleshly system.

[last clause] lead you astray by persuasive talk.

2:8 Christ the Antidote for human philosophy.

2:9 *the fulness—pleroma*—not merely all the qualities of God, as Arius afterwards taught, but the very essence—the nature—of God in all its entirety.

2:10 *complete*—filled full.

2:11 Not the "sins" here as in Romans 6—but the flesh itself.

2:13-14 Jewish legality.

2:14 The receipted bond—all sins settled for.

2:16 Ritualism, asceticism, as in the Essenic Gnostics.

2:18 Pagan mysticism (Persian), superstition, Gnosticism.

2:23 Asceticism—not of any use against the indulgence of the flesh.

3 Christ is *all*.

"Sometimes the loudest proclaimers of the truth are the poorest performers, and so they discount what they say by what they do." —A.T.R.

3:1-4 Risen with Christ.

> 3:2 set—like a watch set to the sun. Four circles:
> vv. 5-11—The inner circle—one's own heart.
> vv. 12-17—Christian fellowship.
> vv. 18-20—The home.
> v. 22—4:6—The world without.

3:5-11 Judgment of the old ways.

3:5 mortify—put to death.

3:8 The habits of the old man—our old clothes, i.e., the man of old—the man you used to be before you knew Christ.

3:12 The habits of the new man—our new clothes.

3:14 [last phrase] "girdle of perfection."

3:15-17 Three rules of conduct.

3:15 rule—umpire.

3:16 Word of Christ—only place in N.T. *psalms*—to strike a note, as on a harp or lyre.

3:18—4:1 Sanctification of natural relationships.

4:2-4 Prayer.

4:5-6 Walk and speech.

4:7-18 Closing salutations. Contrast with Ephesians.

4:16 [last phrase] Probably Ephesians.

4:18 Paul—What would one not give to have this autograph!

New Testament -- 1 Thessalonians – James

1 Thessalonians

The Coming of Christ for His Saints.

The Lord's Return mentioned in every chapter.

1 The child born.

1:1 *in God the Father*—family relationship.

1:2-7 The introduction of the gospel to Thessalonica.

1:7 ensamples—models or types. "Topline believers." See 1 Tim. 4:12.

1:8-10 The effect of the gospel.

1:8 from you sounded out—"God has cast us as bells in His foundry that we may ring." Inglis Fleming.

1:9 The truth of the Lord's Return an incentive to true service—1 Cor. 15:58.

> 1:10 Our Deliverer from the coming wrath:
> The wrath of the Lamb—Rev. 6.
> The wrath of God—Rev. 15, 16.
> The wrath of Satan—Rev. 12.

2 The child nursed.

2:1-13 The manner of the ministry.

2:7 As Moses' mother—Ex. 2:9.

2:14-20 The results of the ministry.

2:19 Reward at the Lord's Return.

Crown of Rejoicing. Connect with Phil. 4:1 and see 2 Tim. 4:8.

3 Pastoral care. The child taught to walk.

3:12-13 Love and holiness to be perfected at the Lord's Return.

4 The child comforted.

4:1-2 Exhortations.

4:13-18 The revelation of the rapture.

4:15 prevent—precede or anticipate.

4:16 rise—stand up.

4:17 meet—To go to meet another in order to return with him. Same as in Acts 28:15.

5 The child taught to fight.

5:1-11 The Day of the Lord.

5:1 Dan. 2:21.

5:12-28 Concluding exhortations and closing salutation.

5:19 The Holy Spirit may be resisted, grieved, quenched.

5:22 All appearances—every form.

2 Thessalonians

The Coming of Christ with His Saints.

1:3-12 Comfort in view of the Lord's Return.

2:1-12 The coming of antichrist. Characteristics of the antichrist—lawlessness, overweening pride, impiety, false miracles.

2:3 *falling away first*—the apostasy.

2:7 *iniquity*—lawlessness—Zech. 5:8.

2:8 *wicked one*—or the lawless one.

2:13-17 The believer's assured hope.

3:1-15 Concluding exhortations.

3:16-17 Closing salutation.

1 Timothy

[Word "some" underscored throughout the letter.]

3:16 godliness—piety.

4:6 Responsibility of a minister of Christ.

4:7-8 The spiritual athlete—2 Tim. 2:5.

4:10 Saviour—Preserver—ch. 6:17; ch. 3:15.

4:12 See 1 Thess. 1:7.

despise—think down on—See Titus 2:15.

4:13-15 Think not only of Paul but of Him who inspired Paul to write.

4:16 continue—"Stay by these things."

2 Timothy

1:7 The spirit of fear—Rom. 8:15.
The spirit of power—Acts 1:8; 1 Thess. 1:5.
The spirit of love—Rom. 5:5; Col. 1:8; 1 Tim. 1:5; 1 Pet. 1:22; Eph. 4:2.
The spirit of a sound mind—1 Cor. 2:10-12; Rom. 12:1.

1:10 *immortality*—incorruptibility.

2:2 A teaching ministry—and the training of others.

2:11-13 One of the earliest Christian hymns.

2:14-21 "The usable preacher."

"God *can* use anyone. But it's up to the preacher not to strain Omnipotence!" A.J.R.

2:14 Not a verbal hairsplitter.

strive not about words—"should not make a war of words."

2:15 A skilled interpreter of the Word of God. "Don't make a crazy quilt out of God's Word." A.J.R.

needeth not to be ashamed—some ought to be but are not. *study*—be zealous.

rightly dividing—cutting straight.

2:16-18 Not Destructive but Constructive.

2:16 shun—step aside. Let the babbler have the road. Do not waste time arguing with him.

2:19-21 A clean vessel.

2:21 "Usable for the Master."

[last part] *prepared*—Ready for every good work.

4:8 The crown of righteousness—See Jas. 1:12.

4:13 *cloke*—Possibly the "book bag."

Titus

1:7 *bishop*—overseer. Elder is the same person.

1:11 1 Pet. 5:2.

2:12 Internal, external, godward.

2:13 *blessed*—happy.
A happy hope because:
Christ Himself is to return.
The first Resurrection and the living changed.
The redemption of the body.
The believer to be rewarded
The earth to be blessed.

2:14 To loose from all bondage to sin.

2:15 *let no man despise you*—"think around you, i.e., outthink you." Dr. A.T.R. See 1 Tim. 4:12.

3:5 Regeneration—See Matt. 19:28.

Philemon

"We are all God's Onesimuses." Luther 1-3 Salutation.

1 Paul—"little."

Philemon—"loving."
Timothy—honored by God.

4-7 Introduction.

8-20 Paul's request for Onesimus.

17 Acceptance.

18 Substitution.

21-25 Closing salutations.

21 Grace exceeds demand.

Hebrews

A Wilderness Epistle. Written to Jews who professed to be Christians—to call them to complete separation from the system of Judaism. The better things of the new covenant contrasted with lesser things of the old. Note the frequent use of the word "better."

1 Christ the Divine Son. Better than angels.
Angels—at creation—Job 38:4-7.
Tested—sin began with angels—a satanic kingdom.
Elect angels—ministering.
Welcomed the Incarnation.
Ministered to Jesus—in the garden—at the Cross—at the
Resurrection—Ascension—Second Coming.
Executors of grace and judgment.

1:3 *image of his person*—exact expression of His character.

1:4 *Being made*—having become.

2 Christ the Sinless Son of Man—lower than angels yet superior to them.

2:1-4 Parenthetical warning.

2:3 "The means that heaven yields must be embraced

And not neglected, else if heaven would
And we will not, heaven's offer we refuse." Shakespeare, *Richard II*, 3:2.

2:8-9 He has been put above everything that all may know everything will be manifestly subjected to Him eventually.

2:10 *perfect*—He was ever perfect in nature, but He had to be perfected as Saviour through His sufferings.

2:11 *are all of one*—one family, one Father, one life.

2:18 Jude 24—He is able to succor—See ch. 7:25.

3 Christ better than Moses—Head over the house of God.

3:7—4:2 Warning.

4:3 Christ better than Joshua (who succeeded Moses and led them into the land).

4:11-13 Warning.

4:14—7:28 Christ better than Aaron—His priesthood superior to the Aaronic.

4:16 [last clause]—for seasonable help.

5:12—6:12 Parenthetical warning.

6:1-2 The "pairs" of O.T.

teaching: *repentance* and *faith*; *baptisms* and *laying on of hands*; resurrection and eternal judgment.

6:13—7:2 8 Christ's Melchisedec priesthood.

6:18 The cities of refuge—See Josh. 20.

7 Christ the true Melchisedec—the King Priest.

7:2 See Isa. 32:17—Righteousness must precede peace.

7:3 The omissions of Scripture are as truly inspired as are its declarations.

7:12 N.B.—"A change of the law!" v. 18; 8:7.

7:25 He is able—ch. 2:18.

8 The new covenant better than the old.

8:6 Better covenant—and better promises.

9—10 The better sacrifice.

9:2 and 4 Note the difference between wherein and which had.

9:8 yet standing—i.e., had a standing before God.

9:12 Eternal redemption.

9:14 Eternal Spirit.

9:15 Eternal inheritance. Death gives validity to a will.

9:22 Peace made by blood—Col. 1:20.
Forgiveness by blood—Eph. 1:7.
Redeemed by blood—1 Pet. 1:18-19.
Justified by blood—Rom. 5:9.
Cleansed by blood—1 John 1:7.
Sanctified by blood—Heb. 13:12.
Overcome by blood—Rev. 12:11.

10:22 Full assurance—Col. 2:2.

10:26-39 Warning.

10:26 *if we sin wilfully*—i.e., he who wilfully rejects the gospel has no other sacrifice.

10:29 *done despite unto*—insulted. Eph. 4:30.

10:35 Reward for service—See ch. 11:24-26.

11 The walk of faith. Witnesses to the power of faith. We do not read, "By faith Lot sat in the gate of Sodom!"
Saving faith—
not: 1—A mere historical faith.
2—Faith in ordinances or sacramental observances.
3—In the Church.
4—In one's self.
5—In experiences.
but: Confidence in what God has revealed. It is grounded in repentance. Christ is its Object. The Word of God is its authority. It is a personal interest in the Lord Jesus Christ.

11:1 *evidence*—assured conviction.

11:17 Note the use of *only begotten*—See John 3:16.

11:21 A worshiper at last instead of a schemer.

11:24 "Providence put Moses into Pharaoh's court— but faith took him out of it." C.H.M.

11:26 Reward for service. See 2 John 8.

11:29 Faith vs. presumption.

11:37 *sawn asunder*—Isaiah is said to have suffered in this way. The walk of faith—Exhortation.

11:5 Note that chastisement is not necessarily punishment. It is education by discipline. One may faint under it—v. 5; or despise it—v. 5, i.e., harden himself against it; or be exercised by it—v. 11. Amos 7:9; Job 34:31.

12:15-17 Warning.

12:17 found no place of repentance—i.e., in the mind of his father.

12:18-24 The two systems contrasted.

12:18-21 Judaism—Deut. 4:10, 11.

12:22-24 Christianity.

12:25-29 Warning.

13 Concluding exhortations.

13:2 Abraham, Lot, Manoah, and others.

13:9 See Col. 3.

13:15 The fruit of the lips—Isa. 57:19.

James

The Work of God *in* us. We do not have the unfoldings of redemption for us here.

The exact place of the Epistle of James is ere the little flock was separated from the Jewish fold— before the Epistle to Hebrews called them out.

1:1 The 12 tribes. Not final rejection yet.

1:4 Connect with 2 Cor. 12:12; Rom. 5:3-5.

1:5 A giving God—Acts 20:35.

1:6 a wave—Motion but no real progress.

1:9 Christian equality—See ch. 2:1-4.

1:12 The crown of life—Rev. 2:10.

1:18 Sovereign grace. Born of the Word of God. 1 Pet. 1:23.

1:25 The will of God should be, for the believer, a law of liberty.

1:26 Empty religion—See Hos. 10:1; Isa. 1:13; 29:8.

2:1 Believers distinguished from the other Jews.

2:2-3 Written at a time when the Church was not yet separated from the synagogue.

2:8-12 Three laws:
The royal law—"Thou shalt love," etc.
"The law"—Ten Commandments.
The law of liberty—the will of God for the believer.

2:12 The law of liberty—See Ps. 119:45.

2:14 Faith works by love—Gal. 5:6.

2:21 justified by works—i.e., before men—"but not before God." Rom. 4.

2:22-26 Faith leads people to do what men of the world cannot understand at all.

3 The tongue: index of what is in the heart. "It is easier to teach others than to govern ourselves." J.N.D.

3:2 *offend all*—all stumble.

4 Addressed to "The 12 Tribes" as such. Struggling to obtain in a carnal way what could be readily given in answer to prayer.

4:3 Prayer—why not answered.

4:4 See Ezek. 16:26.

4:5 [last clause] The Spirit that dwelleth in us jealously yearneth.

4:11 i.e., he is taking the judge's place and accusing the judge of slackness in his dealings.

5:7 Patient—Rev. 3:10; 2 Thess. 3:5.
The Imminence of the Coming:
1—Foreseen by the events in the world.
2—Church.
3—Israel.

5:15 *save the sick*—relieve the exhausted.

New Testament -- 1 Peter – Revelation

1 Peter

The Pilgrim Path.

The journey and its end—suffering and glory.

"The pilgrim's progress from this world to that which is to come." Note the place that "suffering" has in this Epistle.

1 The path through the wilderness.

1:3 Living hope.

1:4 Contrast with Jer. 2:7.

1:8 Christ apprehended by faith which worketh by love.

1:10-12 Prophetic testimony.

1:11 The inspiring Spirit—See 2 Pet. 1:20.

Sufferings of Christ—See ch. 2:19.

1:13-16 Exhortation to steadfastness.

1:17-21 Holiness based on redemption.

1:18 [last part] empty behavior, ancestrally handed down.

1:20 *foreordained*—foreknown.

1:22 Love based on regeneration.

2—4 The Separated life.

2:2 "unto salvation"—J.N.D. and R.V.

2:4-10 The spiritual house and the new priesthood.

2:4 *Living stone*—Matt. 16:18.

2:5 Living stones.

2:11-17 Exhortation. Responsibility to walk in holiness through the world.

2:18—3:7 Sanctified relationships.

2:19 Suffering wrongfully—See v. 20.

2:23 Suffering of Christ—See ch. 3:14.

3:1 without the word—i.e., without nagging.

3:12 Note how the quotation stops in the midst of a sentence—the Day of Judgment not yet come.

3:14 Suffering for righteousness' sake.

3:17-18 Suffering for well-doing—Christ suffered for sins.

4:1 Sufferings of Christ—suffered in the flesh.

4:12 Suffering for Christ's sake.

4:13 Partakers of Christ's sufferings.

4:15 Not to suffer as evildoers.

4:16 Suffering as a Christian.

4:19 Suffering according to the will of God.

5 Service and reward.

5:1 Sufferings of Christ—See v. 10.

5:2 Acts 20:28—Shepherding the flock.

5:7 Ps. 55:22.

5:9 Whom—not which!

5:10 Suffer "a while."

2 Peter

Steadfastness in view of apostasy.

1 Spiritual growth.

1:9 hath forgotten—"Forgetful Green." Bunyan.

1:13 "Stir up"—connect with 2 Cor. 5. See ch. 3:1.

1:19 a more sure word of prophecy—the word of prophecy confirmed.

1:20 any private interpretation—of its own interpretation.

2 Apostate teachers.

2:1 Aspects of perdition.

2:15 Compare with the Epistle of Jude.

3 The Lord's Return.

3:10 The Day of the Lord.

3:12 The Day of God.

3:13 See Isa. 65 and 66.

3:15 Is not Paul's authorship of Hebrews here intimated?

3:16 *hard to be understood*—as in Heb. 6 and 10.

1 John

The Epistle of Fellowship. Light and Love.

In John's Gospel: Eternal Life Manifested in the Son of God.

In first Epistle: Eternal Life Manifested in the Children of God.

1:1 i.e., The beginning of Christianity. Not "in the beginning" as in Gen. 1:1 and John 1:1.

1:2 "The manifested Life."

1:7 Note: It is where we walk—not how. All real Christians walk in the Light.

2:3-11 Obedience the evidence of life.

2:4 He who knows God seeks to obey Him.

2:7-8 See John 12:49—The testimony given by the Father to the Son. The same Life in Him and in us.

2:12-28 The family of God.

2:2 9—3:15 The two families.

3:1 The Father's love for His children.

the sons of God—and such we are. R.V.

3:3 See 1 Thess. 3:12, 13.

3:9 *commit*—practice.

3:16-24 Love, the manifestation of the new nature.

3:17 Active benevolence, a condition of answered prayer. See Prov. 21:13.

3:20-21 The heart may condemn—then real prayer is impossible. See Ps. 66:18.

4:1-6 The spirit of truth and the spirit of error.

4:7-21 Perfect love—its manifestation and results.

4:12 John 1:18—God manifest in us.

4:15 The indwelling God.

4:17 Perfect love.

Day of Judgment—See John 5:24.

5:1-13 Assurance through divine testimony.

5:1-5 Overcomers.

Summary—Love and Obedience overcoming proofs of divine life.

5:6-13 The witness—water for purification, blood for expiation. Others—like the prophets—came by water— proclaiming the Word for cleansing—but He only came by both water and blood. See Ezek. 36:25.

5:14-21 Epilogue.

5:14-15 Confidence. The prayer that God answers.

5:16-17 Sin unto death—Jer. 11:14; Isa. 22:14.

5:18-21 Divine certainties.

2 John

An appendix to 1 John.

Truth to be maintained at all costs.

Only Epistle to a lady.

1 the elect lady—Lady Electra.

3 The Son of the Father—the supreme test.

4-6 Love not inconsistent with loyalty to the truth.

8 Heb. 11:2 6—Reward for service—Rev. 22:12.

10-11 Responsibility to test false teachers and refuse them.

3 John

1 Love ever to be manifested.

8 Fellowship in the truth.

9-11 Warning against ecclesiastical pretension.

Jude

The Increasing Apostasy.

1 See Luke 6:16 as to the relationship of Jude and James, son of Alpheus.

3 The faith once for all delivered.

4 All creeping things were unclean—See Lev. 11:41.

unawares—clandestine work.

5-7 Destruction of apostates.

8-10 Despisers of the truth.

11 Threefold apostasy.

12-13 Divine indictment of evil workers.

14-15 Enoch's prophecy.

16-19 Unholy separatists—Prov. 18:1.

20-23 Faith's resources.

20 Studious, prayerful.

21 Trustful, hopeful.

22-23 Compassionate.

24 Compare with Eph. 3:20.

able—see Heb. 2:18.

The Revelation

The Book of the Throne.

Throne —27 times.

Book of the Lamb. Lamb—24 times.

1:8 See Isa. 48:12.

1:16 See Isa. 49:2.

2:1 John 20:26—Jesus in the midst—See ch. 5:6.

2:2, 9, 19; 3:1, 8, 15 *I know thy works*—the Lord's estimate.

2:4 The greatest heresy of all is the want of love.

2:7, 11 Promise to the overcomer—tree of life—Gen. 3:22.

2:17 Promise—manna—Ex. 16.

White stone—division of the tribes.

2:20 Jezebel—A heathen princess linked to the people of God—the virtual ruler of Israel; Leader in apostasy and seducer of the people. The papal system—1 Kings 16:31.

2:26 Promise—conquest of Canaan.

2:28 Star out of Judah—Balaam's prophecy.

3:5 [first part] Promise—priestly garments.

[last part] See Moses' intercession. Contrast Ps. 69:28.

3:7 The key to the treasury—See Isa. 22:22.

3:9 The conflict with legality. Judaizers in the professed church.

3:12 Promise—the Temple of Solomon.

3:14 Laodicea—A Phrygian city of great wealth—Trading in costly mantles, unguents—Gold pouring in. The Church there largely patterned after the city—self-sufficient, self-reliant, self-righteous.

3:16 Neither enemy nor ardent friend.

3:18 Exhortation—The Lord in the guise of a traveling merchant.

3:20 *Behold, I stand*—what condescension! what patience! *Behold, I knock*—By the Word, By adversity, By bereavement.

4:1 First opening—See ch. 11:19.

4:3 See Ex. 39:10, 13—Sardius—Reuben. Jasper—Benjamin.

4:4 Not king's crowns—but rewards.

4:6 The eyes of the Lord—See Zech. 4:10.

4:11 Man is *for God*; not *God for* man—See Col. 1:18.

5:1 The title deeds—See Jer. 32:10, 11.

5:6 Jesus in the midst—See Matt. 18:20.

6:2 Bloodless victory—the triumphs of peace.

6:4 Internecine and universal warfare.

6:5 Famine—food doled out by weight.

6:8 Pestilence Added to the Horrors of War and Famine.

6:9 Jewish saints slain in the early part of the tribulation.

6:12 See Isa. 2:19, 21. Also Isa. 34:4.

6:13 Collapse of civilization. Downfall of orderly government.

7:2-4 144,000—the remnant of Israel—sealed before the last half of the 70th week begins.

7:9-10 Gentiles who welcome the message of the remnant of Israel in the tribulation days.

8:1 The calm before the coming storm of judgment.

8:3 The angel-priest.

9:2 Strong delusion blotting out the light.

9:7 Nahum 3:17.

9:8 Seductive.

9:10 The prophet that speaketh lies.

10:7 The mystery of God finished when the seventh trumpet sounds.

10:9 Eating the Word of God—Jer. 15:16; Ezek. 2:7; 3:1-3.

10:11 *before*—in respect of.

11:3 The two witnesses. Connect with Zech. 4—Royalty and priesthood.

11:5 See Jer. 5:14.

11:6 A testimony like to that of Moses and Elijah.

11:8 Jerusalem is called Sodom—See Isa. 1:10.

11:12 The mid-tribulation rapture of the witnesses who are slain under the beast.

11:15 The seventh trumpet ushers in the Kingdom and goes on to the judgment of the wicked, i.e., to the Great White Throne, thus completing a prophetic series.

11:19 Second *opening*—See ch. 15:5.

12 A "Sign" in Heaven—God's thoughts of Israel. Jer. 4:31—See Isa. 66:7. The woman is not in heaven—but on the earth as verse 12 proves. Israel the mother of the Messiah—See Isa. 9:6; Mic. 4:10; 5:2, 3; Rom. 9-5.

12:2 See full description of this same scene in Micah 4:8 to 13.

12:14 The eagle—Ex. 19:4.

13:2 The nondescript beast of Dan. 7:7.

13:3 The imperial head wounded to death—but revived by satanic power. The imperial head once wounded to death, shall rise again in the last days—See Hab. 3:13.

13:11 The lamb-like beast—the false Messiah. See Dan. 11:36 to 45; 2 Thess. 2; 1 John 2.

13:15 *life*—breath. Contrast Hab. 2:19.

14:11 See Isa. 34:10.

14:13 *Blessed*—See ch. 16:15. "The returns are not all in yet!" W. P. White.

14:14 The Son of Man—last use of the term—See Matt. 8:20.

14:15 The harvest—discriminative judgment—See Matt. 13:30.

14:18 The vintage—Joel 3:13. The unsparing judgment of apostate Israel.

15:2 The saints slain in the great tribulation.

15:5 Third *opening*—see ch. 19:11.

16:1 *vials*—bowls.—Compare the judgments of the bowls with the plagues of Egypt.

16:12 The eastern confederation, "The kings of the sunrising."

16:15 *Blessed*—Seech. 19:9.

17:5 Who are the daughters? See Ezek. 16:44.

18:7 Babylon's proud boast—See Isa. 47:7.

18:14 "The fruit season of thy soul's desire has gone from thee."

19:9 *Blessed*—See ch. 20:6.

19:11 Fourth *opening*.

19:15-16 The winepress—See Isa. 63:1-10.

20:6 Blessed—See ch. 22:7.

20:11 Job 14:12.

20:25 Contrast Ezek. 42.

22:1 The river of God—See Gen. 2:10; Ps. 36:8; 46:4; 65:9; Cant. 4:15; Isa. 58:11; Ezek. 47:1-12.

22:7 *Blessed*—see v. 14.

22:10 Contrast with Daniel 12. See Isa. 29:10-12.

22:12 Reward at the judgment seat of Christ. See 2 John 8; Isa. 40:10; 62:11.

22:14 *do His commandments*—"wash their robes," correct reading.

Made in the USA
Coppell, TX
21 June 2023

18369005R00111